To the
love of my life
I am yours till the
end of time. x x x
x x x
Pam
20.08.05

C000252406

Flies, Flowers, Fur & Feather

A guide to the waterside flowers, flies and
artificial flies of interest to the fisherman

John Cawthorne

The Crowood Press

First published in 2002 by
The Crowood Press Ltd
Ramsbury, Marlborough
Wiltshire SN8 2HR

British Library Cataloguing-in-Publication Data

A catalogue record for this book is available from the British Library.

ISBN 1 86126 550 6

To
William Francis Cawthorne
when one word was worth a thousand pictures

For
Anne, William, Peter and Carole

Many thanks to Carol, Jack Shardlow, Tom Richardson, Sean Feeney, Stephen Moores, Mary Jones and Wilf Skelton. Thanks also to Matthew Fletcher

Designed and edited by Focus Publishing, Sevenoaks, Kent

Printed and bound in Singapore by Craft Print International Ltd

With many thanks to Stephen Moores and Sean Feeney, my friends and riverkeepers on the Wye and Derwent, for all their help and advice and for always making us welcome, whatever the circumstances. I am continually in the debt of my good friend and now 'part-time' fishing partner, adviser and fly-tier, Jack Shardlow, for his continued help and support. Also, my thanks go to Wilf Skelton, my full-time fishing partner, helper and continual distracter, who has become my right hand in everything I do. I would also like to thank Tom Richardson, without whom the Wye would not be the wonderful river that it is.

Acknowledgements

A little knowledge is not in fact a dangerous thing, for without the pieces of knowledge the complete picture is never achieved. Throughout the history of fly fishing, knowledge has been gained, passed down and added to, and conclusions have been arrived at. At one time there was no knowledge of the link between the crawling cased caddis and the winged adult, no understanding that one dull fly could transform itself into such a bright, shiny fly by discarding one set of wings and body for another in a matter of seconds. There was no knowledge that one creature living fully in water could transform itself into a totally different creature living fully in the air, nor that fish travelled thousands of miles in order to deposit their eggs in the rivers of their birth. All this knowledge has had to be continually sought out and verified. From the times of Walton and Cotton, down through the works of Ronalds, Halford, Skues and Marriot, Courtney Williams and Harris, up to the present day with men like Price, Roberts, Edwards, Jardine, O'Reilly and Goddard and Clarke, our knowledge of our sport is being continually widened. To these men – and indeed all the unsung fishermen who have added to our knowledge – we are all indebted. Without their interest and ability to pass knowledge on to others a book of this nature would not be possible.

Contents

Introduction

The image projected by fly fishermen as time goes by will become more and more important, as we will have to demonstrate that we are sensitive to and aware of every aspect of our countryside. We will need to show that the first and utmost thought in our minds is not the desire to catch more and more fish but that the pleasure fly fishing gives us is due to our observance of and regard for the countryside and the natural laws that govern it. We shall continually need to stress that many areas of water, whether rivers or lakes, are in the clean and cared-for state they are in solely because of the continued interest and attention of the fly fisherman. I, like many others, have no interest in being merely engaged in the pursuit of trout in some sterile environment where the fisherman, and the revenue made from him, is the main concern.

First in our priorities must be the environment and, in the case of our river valleys particularly, a healthy environment needs a pure and unpolluted watercourse. Indeed healthy bankside vegetation is totally dependent on this. Invertebrate life, on which most other wildlife directly or indirectly depends, is totally reliant on water quality and its purity. Both large animals and plants rely on a plentiful, healthy supply of insects, as indeed do the fish. The importance of the fisherman should come well down the list when considering the natural cycle, and rightly so. How often, however, do we hear such comments as 'the banks are getting out of hand, there are too many overhanging trees', or 'there are certain parts of this river you cannot get a rod into'? Well, isn't this really how it should be? All wildlife, fish and insects need places to rest in; surely we, as fishermen, don't need to take every square foot of the place for ourselves! Don't those hard-to-fish, overgrown areas merely add to the required skill and enjoyment we feel as anglers?

I am very fortunate in that I fish with two people who enjoy all aspects of the countryside as much as they do their fishing. Both Jack and Wilf will readily break off from their fishing pursuits to look at some animal, bird or plant of particular interest. We mostly fish the rivers Wye and Derwent on the Chatsworth Estate in Derbyshire, two valleys full of contrast. The Wye is narrow and very intimate, the Derwent wider and more open. Both rivers are for the most part pure, clean and teeming with life. The valleys, which are in parts SSSIs, are looked after by two of the friendliest and competent river keepers you could wish to meet, namely Stephen Moores and Sean Feeney. They are not, thankfully, solely interested in the well-being, or the catch accounts, of the fishing members, but also in the care and maintenance of the whole river environment. An awareness that every part comes together to make up the whole and that the whole is not stable without every part has to be the fundamental thinking of everyone who enjoys and participates in countryside pursuits.

I find it very difficult to explain my addiction to flyfishing. I think the answer lies somewhere in the feeling I get, especially when fishing with something that imitates a natural fly, of having to adapt both manner and ways to become a part of the environment that I enjoy so much. I once read, in an article in a leading angling magazine, a quote by a so-called leading exponent of the art of flyfishing: 'Anyone who says he goes fly fishing for any other reason than to catch fish is a liar'. Well, thankfully, I have surrounded myself with such 'liars' and their continued friendship and support have made this book possible – for it is not only about catching fish but also about the insects and plants we are likely to see in the pursuit of our gentle art.

PART 1

The Upwinged Flies

Ephemeroptera

The *Ephemeroptera* are the main group of flies of interest to the fisherman. They range from the small *Caenis* to the Mayfly. They have all been given fisherman's names to describe them and these names over the years have become accepted along with their Latin counterparts. Some of the names relate to the time of hatch of the adult fly – March Brown, Mayfly and so on. Others relate to the colour of the insect – Large Dark Olive, Yellow May Dun – while others refer to the locations where they are most likely to be found – Pond Olive, Ditch Dun and so on. As these names have become accepted other names have been discarded to save confusion.

Unlike most other insects, the *Ephemeroptera* cannot fold their wings backwards over the body, and this results in their most obvious characteristic when at rest and the common collective name of upwinged flies. Although they do not have the obvious colours of many of the winged insects, such as butterflies and moths for example, their fine transparent wings and delicate bodies give them a more subdued beauty. A large hatch of Mayflies is a wonderful sight, and to see trout watching and feeding on them continues to fascinate any fly fisherman.

The following section shows the female dun of each species of interest to the fisherman along with the type of larva. The identification of larvae to species is very difficult; it is much simpler to match them to families, and for fishing purposes this is quite adequate. Along with the illustrations of the naturals are shown suggested artificials of both dun and nymph. The recipes are given in the text along with the name of the designer where known.

Autumn Dun
Ecdyonorus dispar (Plate 1)

The Autumn Dun is a late summer fly usually seen from August onwards and was, at one time, called the August Dun. In colouring and size it is similar to the March Brown and Late March Brown although the wings do not have the same dark mottling. Unlike most of the stone-clinger type nymphs this fly can be found on larger lakes as well as the spate rivers. The egg-laying female will seek out a suitable stone in the shallows and, pushing her abdomen through the water surface, deposit her eggs on the sides of the stone.

Nymph:
Size:	Up to 15mm
Colour:	Fawn-brown
Type:	Stone-clinger

Adult:
Size:	Up to 13mm
Colour:	Dun: Female: yellowish-brown abdomen with rich brown markings down the sides, fawn wings with brown veins, olive-brown legs, red-brown eyes, grey tails Male: As female but with dark green-brown eyes Spinner: Female: rich red-brown abdomen, bright wings with clear brown veins, olive-brown legs, red-brown eyes and tails. Male: As female
Habitat	Spate rivers and stony lakes
Distribution:	Ireland, areas of Wales, the West Country and northern England
Time of day:	Any time of day
Time of year:	Late July–October, but mostly August–September
Shape of rear wing:	Large, upright coastal projections

Dressings

1. August Dun (Woolley)

DRESSING

Hook length: 13mm
Thread: Yellow
Tail: Brown hackle fibres
Abdomen: Brown floss
Rib: Yellow floss
Wing: Mottled fawn hen pheasant feather
Hackle: Brown cock

2. Autumn Dun Floating Nymph (Jardine)

DRESSING

Hook length: 15mm
Thread: Yellow
Tail: Ginger feather fibres
Abdomen: Fawn antron
Rib: Yellow thread
Emerging wing: Antron floss
Legs: Golden olive cock

3. August Dun Nymph (Roberts)

DRESSING

Hook length: 15mm
Thread: Yellow
Tail: Yellow fibres from a guinea fowl
Abdomen: Yellow and brown seal's fur sub
Rib: Gold wire
Hackle: Golden plover feather

Plate 1

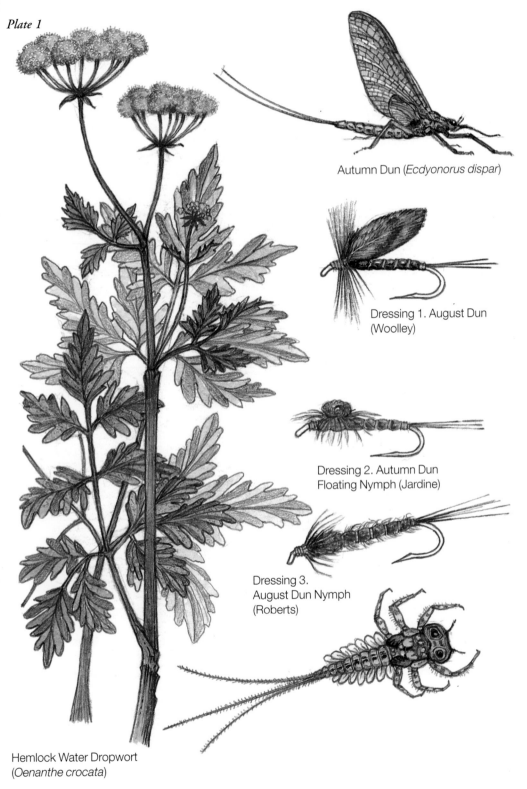

Autumn Dun (*Ecdyonorus dispar*)

Dressing 1. August Dun
(Woolley)

Dressing 2. Autumn Dun
Floating Nymph (Jardine)

Dressing 3.
August Dun Nymph
(Roberts)

Hemlock Water Dropwort
(*Oenanthe crocata*)

Hemlock Water Dropwort
Oenanthe crocata (Plate 1)
Carrot family (*Umbelliferae*)

Flower head:	Numerous white flowers carried in rounded umbels on tall, hollow, many-branched stems
Leaves:	Each leaf is made up of 2–4 pairs of fern-like leaflets
Flowering time:	May–September
Height:	Up to 1.5m
Habit:	Native perennial
Habitat:	Wet places, marshes, streams and rivers
Distribution:	Widespread and common except eastern England, northern Scotland and central Ireland
General:	A pleasantly scented plant that is and looks like a wild member of the carrot and parsley family. Here the resemblance stops, as it is an extremely poisonous plant in all its parts; if eaten, death may, and has, occurred within three hours. It is often found growing in large, dense clumps by the sides of rivers and streams

Blue-Winged Olive
Ephemerella ignita (Plate 2)

The Blue-Winged Olive, although having a preference for the more heavily weeded streams and rivers, can also be found in still waters and smaller streams containing less vegetation. Where it occurs, particularly on weeded rivers such as chalk streams, the hatches can be heavy, particularly towards early evening. After mating it is not unusual to see large numbers of female spinners over the water surface. The fact that spinners and duns can be found in large numbers on the water surface at the same time adds to the trout's obvious interest in this particular olive. Another observation recorded by some experts is that the dun appears to take a longer than normal time to escape from the nymphal skin.

Nymph:	
Size:	Up to 12mm
Colour:	Yellow-brown with darker brown markings, legs with dark and light bands
Type:	Moss- and weed-crawler
Adult:	
Size:	Up to 10mm
Colour:	Dun: Female: olive-green abdomen, smoke-grey wings, olive-green legs, very dark green eyes, grey tails
	Male: orange-brown abdomen, smoke-grey wings, orange-brown legs, red eyes, olive-grey tails
	Spinner: Female: orange-brown abdomen, bright wings with pale yellow-brown veins, pale orange-brown legs, dark olive eyes, pale-grey tails
	Male: dark, rich-brown

Plate 2

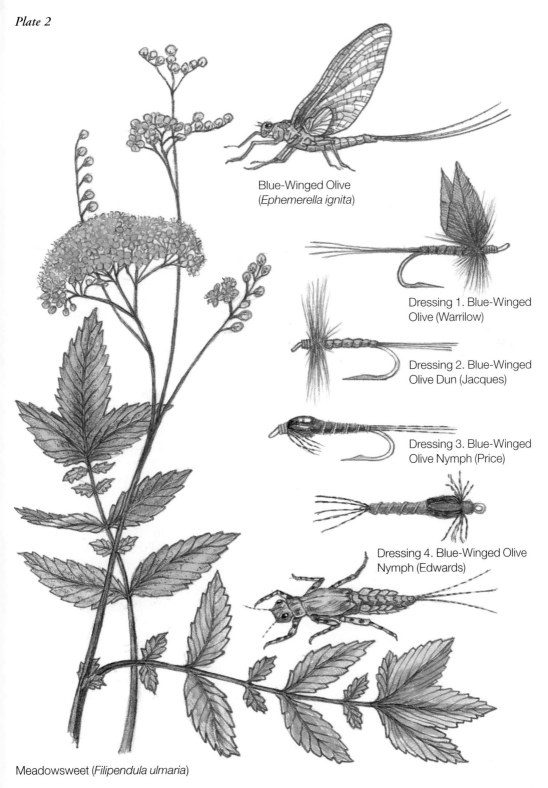

Blue-Winged Olive
(*Ephemerella ignita*)

Dressing 1. Blue-Winged
Olive (Warrilow)

Dressing 2. Blue-Winged
Olive Dun (Jacques)

Dressing 3. Blue-Winged
Olive Nymph (Price)

Dressing 4. Blue-Winged Olive
Nymph (Edwards)

Meadowsweet (*Filipendula ulmaria*)

abdomen, bright wings with pale-brown veins, brown legs, red eyes, brown tails

Habitat: Rivers, particularly those with good weed growth, streams and some still waters

Distribution: Common throughout most of the British Isles

Time of day: Usually after midday until dark

Time of year: May–September

Shape of rear wing: Upright with coastal projection

Meadowsweet
Filipendula ulmaria (**Plate 2**)
Rose family (*Rosaceae*)
(Queen of the Meadows, Bittersweet, Sweet Hay, Summer's Farewell)

Flower head: Strongly scented tiny white flowers carried in umbels on erect, angular stems which are often branched at the top ▶

Dressings

1. Blue-Winged Olive (Warrilow)

DRESSING
Hook length: 10mm
Thread: Olive
Tail: Olive cock fibres
Abdomen: Goose herl brown-olive
Rib: Olive thread
Wing: Dark-dun feathers
Hackle: Olive cock

2. Blue-Winged Olive Dun (Jacques)

DRESSING
Hook length: 10mm
Thread: Orange
Tail: Dark-olive cock fibres
Abdomen: Olive PVC over olive ostrich herls
Hackle: Dark-olive cock

3. Blue-Winged Olive Nymph (Price)

DRESSING
Hook length: 12mm
Thread: Olive
Tail: Olive grizzle cock
Abdomen: Olive fur or antron
Rib: Transparent olive swannundaze
Thorax: Olive fur or antron
Wing pads: Slips to shape cut from recording tape
Wingcase: Recording tape over thorax
Legs: Partridge dyed olive

4. Blue-Winged Olive Nymph (Edwards)

DRESSING
Hook length: 10mm
Thread: Orange
Tail: Mottled partridge
Abdomen: Sandy-coloured hare's ear fur
Rib: Gold wire
Thorax: Sandy hare's ear fur
Wingcase: Pheasant tail fibres tied either side of thorax area leaving strip of thorax fur showing above
Legs: Marked partridge feather

▶ Individual flowers are up to 1cm wide

Leaves: The main stem leaves consist of 2–5 pairs of large leaflets with smaller leaflets in between. The leaflets are deeply divided and serrated with a covering of silvery hairs on the undersides and reddish veins. Their first appearance is in spring when a ground rosette of leaves begins to emerge

Flowering time: June–August

Height: Up to 1.5m

Habit: Native perennial

Habitat: Wet places, meadows, banks of rivers, streams and water meadows.

Distribution: Common throughout.

General: Meadowsweet, which was a favourite plant of Elizabeth I, has had many uses throughout history. In mediaeval times it was frequently strewn on floors to keep a room smelling sweetly – both the leaves and flowers are highly scented but each gives off a different scent. In Ireland, Meadowsweet was used to scour out old milk churns, whilst the Anglo-Saxons used it to flavour mead and beer. Culpepper said that the leaves added to a glass of claret would add relish. Medicinally, Meadowsweet was effective against malaria, colds and influenza, and also as an anti-rheumatic. It was from the flower heads of Meadowsweet that in 1839 salyalic acid was discovered – this was later synthesized to enable the production of aspirin

Angler's Curse, Broadwing
Caenis (Plate 3)

This is a group of six species of very small flies, hence the common name of Angler's Curse. Due to the size and difficulty of identification, so far as the angler is concerned they are treated as one. The small size and, at times, the vast numbers of flies available to the trout make it a very difficult fly to have any success with. The nymph is a bottom-dweller and so small that it is almost impossible to tie a copy that will be heavy enough to fish at the correct depth. Because of the nymph's habit of dwelling in the silt, its body often becomes covered in the silt or detritus and I have seen individuals that have been almost white; this may explain why some of the patterns vary so much in colour. Another point to note is that although you can buy Caenis Nymphs on size 16, and even 14 hooks, they cannot possibly be copies of the natural nymphs as the actual hook size needed would be more like a size 20, 4 or 5mm.

The lifespan of the adult is very short – from emergence to dead spinner can be a matter of 90 minutes or less. Because of the short lifespan, every stage of the insect is available to the trout at the same time, which poses another problem in choice of artificial, emerging nymph, dun or spinner. Some anglers will tell you at this point you should go home but perseverance is its own reward, and a small Goddard's Last Hope, or small parachute Grey Duster will at times give results.

Nymph:

Size: Up to 6mm

Colour: Light brown with darker brown markings

Type: Silt dweller

Adult:

Size: Up to 5mm

Plate 3

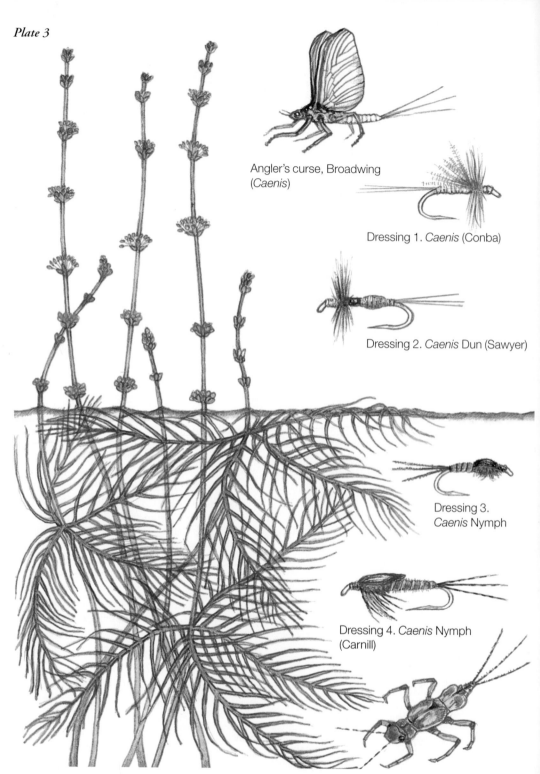

Angler's curse, Broadwing
(*Caenis*)

Dressing 1. *Caenis* (Conba)

Dressing 2. *Caenis* Dun (Sawyer)

Dressing 3.
Caenis Nymph

Dressing 4. *Caenis* Nymph
(Carnill)

Spiked Water Milfoil (*Myriophyllum spicatum*)

Colour: Dun: Female: cream abdomen, brown thorax area, grey wing, pale-grey legs, dark-brown eyes, white tails
Male: as female
Spinner: as duns but with a lighter body and bright wings, and longer tails. In the male this can be very obvious, the tail being three times the length of the body
Habitat: Rivers and lakes with silty bottoms
Distribution: Common
Time of day: Morning or afternoon
Time of year: May–September
Shape of rear wing: None

Spiked Water Milfoil
Myriophyllum spicatum (Plate 3)
Water Milfoil family (*Haloragaceae*)

Flower head: Tiny red flowers carried in whorls of 4 on a spike which emerges above the water. The lower flowers are female, the upper ones male – each flower has 4 stamens
Leaves: Dark green leaves in whorls of 4–6 carried below the surface on wine red stems. Feathery in appearance
Flowering time: June–July

Dressings

1. *Caenis* (Conba)

DRESSING

Hook length: 5mm
Thread: White
Tail: White feather fibres
Abdomen: White thread
Wing: White cul-de-canard
Hackle: White cock

2. *Caenis* Dun (Sawyer)

DRESSING

Hook length: 5mm
Thread: White
Tail: Cream cock fibres
Abdomen: Mole fur
Thorax: Ostrich herl stripped, tied shiny side outwards
Hackle: Short blue-dun

3. *Caenis* Nymph

DRESSING

Hook length: 6mm
Thread: Brown
Tail: Three short cock-pheasant fibres spaced apart
Abdomen: Grey-brown fur
Rib: Brown thread
Thorax: Grey-brown fur picked out for legs
Wingcase: Dark pheasant tail fibres over thorax

4. *Caenis* Nymph (Carnill)

DRESSING

Hook length: 6mm
Thread: Brown
Tail: Three brown partridge fibres spaced apart
Abdomen: Heron herl
Rib: Stripped peacock quill
Thorax: Hare's ear
Wingcase: Heron quill cut to shape to go halfway down the abdomen
Legs: Fibres from a partridge hackle

13

Height:	Up to 3m
Habit:	Perennial
Habitat:	Ponds, lakes, pools and slow-moving rivers and streams
Distribution:	Common throughout
General:	In the wild this plant is found growing in areas that are rich in chalk, while as a cultivated species it is widely used in aquaria and ornamental ponds. It can grow so prolifically that it chokes up small ponds or lakes, especially in summer. *Myriophyllum* is taken from the Greek *myrios*, meaning many and *phyllon*, meaning 'leaf', referring to the plant's numerous submerged feathery leaves

Claret Dun
Leptaphlebia vespertina
(Plate 4)

The Claret Dun, although mostly a fly of acidic still waters, such as moorland lakes, is also to be found on slow-flowing rivers and upland streams of a peaty nature. It is one of the few flies with very dark colouration, the other obvious example being the Iron Blue, a fly that it could be confused with. The two obvious differences are the number of tails, the Claret Dun having three, the Iron Blue only having two. Another difference, and a peculiarity to the Claret Dun, is the contrasting colouration of the paler hindwings to the darker forewings. The nymphs of the *Leptophlebia* have gills made up of two long filaments and longer than normal tails.

| Nymph: | |
| Size: | Up to 12mm |

Colour:	Yellow-brown to reddish-brown
Type:	Laboured swimmer
Adult:	
Size:	Up to 10mm
Colour:	Dun: Female: dark red-brown, almost black, abdomen, grey-black main wing, noticeably grey-fawn hindwing, brown-black legs, black eyes, brown-black tails Male: as female but with red-brown eyes Spinner: Female: rich dark-brown abdomen, bright wings with light-brown veins, medium brown legs, dark red-brown eyes, pale-brown tails Male: as female
Habitat:	Still and slow-flowing acidic water
Distribution:	Localized throughout British Isles especially in some of Ireland's moorland loughs
Time of day:	Midday onwards
Time of year:	April–mid-July
Shape of rear wing:	Upright with coastal projections

Dressings

1. Claret Dun (Harris)

DRESSING

Hook length: 10mm
Thread: Claret
Tail: Dark blue-dun cock fibres
Abdomen: Heron herl dyed claret
Rib: Gold wire
Hackle: Dark blue-dun – the bottom of the hackle is cut with a 'V'

Plate 4

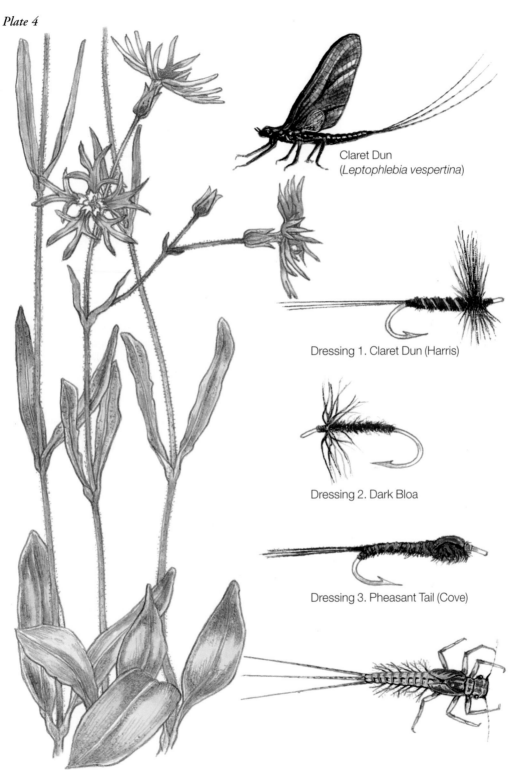

Claret Dun
(*Leptophlebia vespertina*)

Dressing 1. Claret Dun (Harris)

Dressing 2. Dark Bloa

Dressing 3. Pheasant Tail (Cove)

Ragged Robin (*Lychnis flos-cuculi*)

2. Dark Bloa

DRESSING

Hook length: 12mm
Thread: Claret
Abdomen: Claret seal's fur sub
Hackle: Black hen

3. Pheasant Tail (Cove)

DRESSING

Hook length: 12mm
Thread: Brown
Tail: Pheasant tail fairly long
Abdomen: Pheasant tail
Rib: Copper wire
Thorax: Rabbit fur
Wingcase: Pheasant tail over thorax

Ragged Robin
Lychnis flos-cuculi (Plate 4)
Pink family (*Caryophyllaceae*)
(Indian Pink, Billy Buttons, Rough Robin, Bachelor's Buttons)

Flower head:	Pinky-mauve flowers, occasionally white, 20–25mm across and carried in loose branched clusters. The five petals are deeply divided into four narrow segments giving rise to a 'ragged' appearance
Leaves:	Carried in opposite pairs. The lower leaves are oblong and stalked, whilst the upper are more lance-shaped
Flowering time:	May–August
Height:	Up to 75cm

Habit:	Native perennial
Habitat:	Marshes, damp meadows and woods, stream and river banks
Distribution:	Common throughout
General:	This characteristic plant of water meadows avoids acid conditions. Its name *flos-cuculi* is derived from the Latin for 'cuckoo flower', a name shared with other flowers. It is one of the plants often visited by leaf-hopper insects in order to extract juices from it. When the juices combine with saliva from the insect a froth is formed, which was often thought to be the work of the devil

Dark Olive Dun
Baetis atrebatinus (Plate 5)

The Dark Olive is a fairly localized fly found in calcareous rivers of Ireland and southern and northern England. Although very similar to *Baetis rhodani*, the Large Dark Olive, it is slightly smaller and the hindwing is without the small coastal projection. Hatches are small and usually in the early and late part of the fishing season.

Nymph:	
Size:	Up to 12mm
Colour:	Olive-brown
Type:	Agile darter

Adult:	
Size:	Up to 10mm
Colour:	Dun: Female: olive-brown abdomen, grey-brown wings, pale olive-brown legs, red-brown eyes, grey tails

Male: as female
Spinner: Female: rich red-brown abdomen with pale segmentation, bright wings with pale-brown veins, pale-olive legs, dark-brown eyes, pale-olive tails
Male: as female but with olive abdomen with last three segments orange-brown

Habitat: Calcareous streams and rivers
Distribution: Localized throughout Britain and Ireland
Time of day: Midday
Time of year: May–October
Shape of rear wing: Small, oval

Dressings

1. Dark Olive Dun (Clegg)

DRESSING

Hook length: 10mm
Thread: Olive
Tail: Dark-olive cock fibres
Abdomen: Dubbed dark-olive wool
Rib: Thin, white DRF floss
Hackle: Blue-dun and dark-olive cock wound together

2. Dark Olive Nymph (Leisenring)

DRESSING

Hook length: 12mm
Thread: Primrose
Tail: Blue-dun cock hackle fibres
Abdomen: Olive seal's fur sub and brown hair mixed
Rib: Gold wire
Thorax: As abdomen
Legs: Dark dun hen

3. Dark Olive Nymph (Hanna)

DRESSING

Hook length: 12mm
Thread: Brown
Tail: Dark-olive cock
Abdomen: Olive seal's fur
Rib: Gold wire
Thorax: As abdomen
Wingcase: Cock pheasant over abdomen
Legs: Olive cock

Butterwort
Pinguicula vulgaris (Plate 5)
Butterwort family (*Lentibulariaceae*)
(Bog Violet)

Flower head: Solitary, bluish-violet flower, 1–2cm across with lightish throat, carried on a long, leafless stem. Each flower has two lips. The lobes of the lower lip slightly overlap and are longer than they are broad. The top lip is slightly curved upwards. There is a long, sharply pointed spur, 5–6mm in length, which is either straight or slightly curved
Leaves: A basal rosette of yellowish-green, fleshy leaves, oval to oblong in shape, with untoothed, curled edges and sticky surfaces
Flowering time: May–July
Height: Up to 15cm
Habit: Native perennial
Habitat: Mountain areas, wet heaths, rocks and bogs

Plate 5

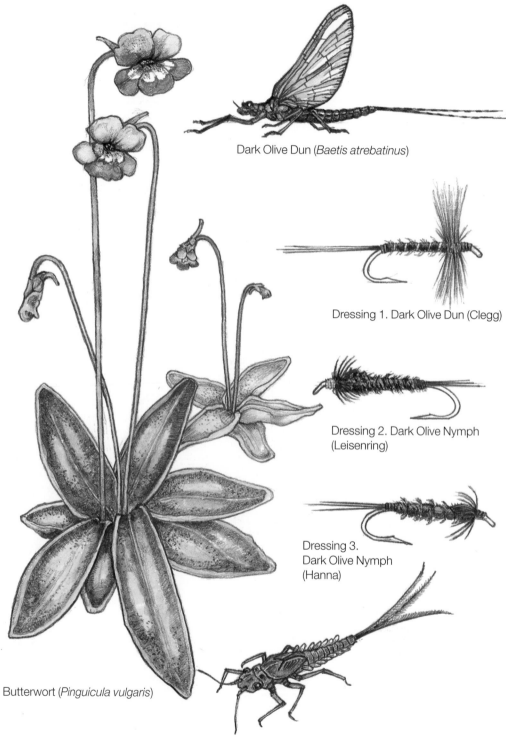

Dark Olive Dun (*Baetis atrebatinus*)

Dressing 1. Dark Olive Dun (Clegg)

Dressing 2. Dark Olive Nymph
(Leisenring)

Dressing 3.
Dark Olive Nymph
(Hanna)

Butterwort (*Pinguicula vulgaris*)

Distribution:	Throughout Britain, but uncommon in southern Britain and southern Ireland
General:	Butterwort is a native carnivorous perennial which overwinters as a rootless bud. Sticky glands on the leaf surfaces trap insects and their struggling activates a mechanism that causes the leaves to curl up and so trap their prey. Enzymes are then secreted onto the insect to digest it and mineral salts are extracted into the plant. The remains are then blown away or washed away by rain when the leaf reopens. The name *Pinguicula* derives from the Latin *pinguin* meaning 'fat' – this alludes to the greasy appearance of the leaves. It is thought that the plant may once have been used to curdle milk for making butter, hence the name 'Butterwort'. Milk from cows that have eaten Butterwort was supposedly good for a newborn child. The plant itself was allegedly useful in the protection against witches and fairies

Ditch Dun
Habrophlebia fusca (Plate 6)

The Ditch Dun is fairly limited in its distribution and, as the name suggests, is a fly of slow-moving water. The adult has three tails and a colouration similar to the Iron Blue, the Iron Blue having only two tails. Because of their limited distribution and location very few patterns have been devised. The nymph is a laboured swimmer and, over its length, slightly broader than the agile darters. The gills are narrow and reasonably long. Because of the locations in which the Ditch Dun is found it is of limited value to the fisherman.

Nymph:	
Size:	Up to 10mm
Colour:	Rich brown
Type:	Laboured swimmer
Adult:	
Size:	Up to 8mm
Colour:	Dun: Female: dull olive abdomen, dull grey wings, olive-grey legs, dull green eyes
	Male: olive-grey abdomen, dull-grey wings, olive-grey legs, dull-red eyes
	Spinner: Female: rich-brown abdomen, transparent wings with brown veins, olive legs, green eyes
	Male: as female but with dull red eyes
Habitat:	Very slow-moving water
Distribution:	Very localized, England and Wales
Time of day:	Midday
Time of year:	June–September
Shape of rear wing:	Large with coastal projection

Dressings

1. Ditch Dun (Kite)

DRESSING

Hook length: 8mm
Thread: Purple
Tail: Blue-dun fibres
Abdomen: Heron herls
Rib: Gold wire
Thorax: Heron herls as abdomen but darker
Hackle: Blue-dun cock dark

2. Pheasant Tail Nymph (Sawyer)

DRESSING

Hook length: 10mm
Thread: Copper wire
Tail: Cock pheasant fibres
Abdomen: Copper wire underneath to shape then copper wire and pheasant tail fibres wound together over.
Wingcase: Pheasant tail fibres doubled over thorax area

3. Ditch Dun Nymph (Kite)

DRESSING

Hook length: 10mm
Thread: Purple
Tail: Blue-dun fibres
Abdomen: Heron herls
Rib: Gold wire
Thorax: Heron herl built up slightly over weighted thorax
Legs: Blue-dun fibres under thorax

Arrowhead
Sagittaria sagittifolia (Plate 6)
Water Plantain family
(*Alismataceae*)

Flower head:	White flowers made up of 3 sepals, 3 petals and a large number of purple anthers. Bases of the petals are tinged violet, up to 2cm in diameter. Flowers are carried in whorls around an erect, unbranched stem which is triangular in cross-section. Both male and female flowers are present on the same plant, male flowers being higher up the stem than female
Leaves:	Aerial leaves carried above the water at the end of long stems have a very distinctive arrow-shaped blade, untoothed margins and a glossy appearance. Ribbon-like, submerged leaves are also present and occasionally also elliptical, long-stalked floating leaves. All leaves are basal
Fruit:	One-seeded, 4–6cm long forming a globe-shaped burr-like head
Flowering time:	July–August
Height:	Up to 90cm
Habit:	Perennial
Habitat:	Still or slow-moving shallow water, rich in nutrients
Distribution:	Fairly common but localized in England. Rarer elsewhere
General:	Arrowhead is a native semi-aquatic, hairless plant frequently found in landscaped water gardens where it is much used because of its very striking ▶

Plate 6

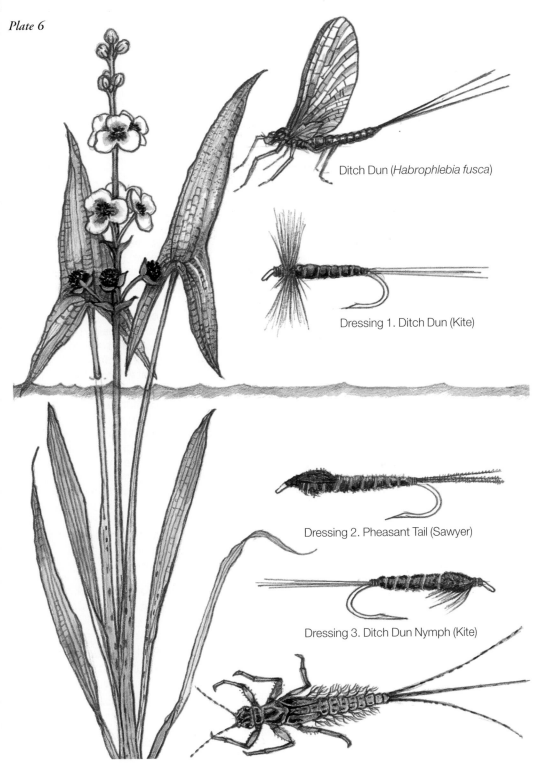

Ditch Dun (*Habrophlebia fusca*)

Dressing 1. Ditch Dun (Kite)

Dressing 2. Pheasant Tail (Sawyer)

Dressing 3. Ditch Dun Nymph (Kite)

Arrowhead (*Sagittaria sagittifolia*)

21

▶ and distinctive appearance. Its name is derived from Latin, *Sagittarius* meaning armed with arrows, and is a direct reference to the unmistakable shape of its aerial leaves. Although of no medicinal use, Arrowhead is cultivated in parts of Asia, especially China, as a foodstuff – it has edible, fleshy roots. A closely related species, *Sagittaria latifolia*, was also cultivated for its roots by native American Indians and was known to the early settlers as Duck Potato. This latter species is now naturalized in parts of Europe

Dusky Yellowstreak
Heptagenia lateralis (Plate 7)

This upwinged fly, although widespread over the country from Scotland through part of England down as far as Devon and Ireland, is nevertheless localized in its distribution. The Dusky Yellowstreak nymph is a stone-clinger while the fly prefers spate rivers, streams and upland lakes. The nymph, when about to emerge into the dun, will seek out stones in the shallower areas of the lake or river. This is partly because of the unique nature of the emergence. The dun breaks free from the shuck underwater and emerges fully formed at the surface, where it then takes time to dry its wings before flying off. The most obvious point of identification of the adult is the two yellow marks on either side of the front thorax area, which give the fly its name.

Nymph:		
Size:		Up to 12mm
Colour:		Fawn-brown, very few markings
Type:		Stone-clinger
Adult:		
Size:		Up to 10mm
Colour:		Dun: Female: olive-brown abdomen, dark-grey wings, olive-brown legs, brown-black eyes, grey tails
		Male: as female
		Spinner: Female: amber-brown abdomen, bright wings with brown veins, olive-brown legs, brown-black eyes, pale brown tails
		Male: as female
		All duns and spinners have two yellow marks either side of front thorax area
Habitat:		Spate rivers, streams and upland lakes with stony bottoms
Distribution:		Localized throughout Britain and Ireland
Time of day:		After midday
Time of year:		May–September
Shape of rear wing:		Upright with coastal projection

Dressings

1. Dusky Yellowstreak (Roberts)

DRESSING

Hook length: 10mm
Thread: Brown
Tail: Blue-dun cock fibres
Abdomen: Grey herls
Rib: Brown thread
Hackle: Blue-dun and grizzle wound together

Plate 7

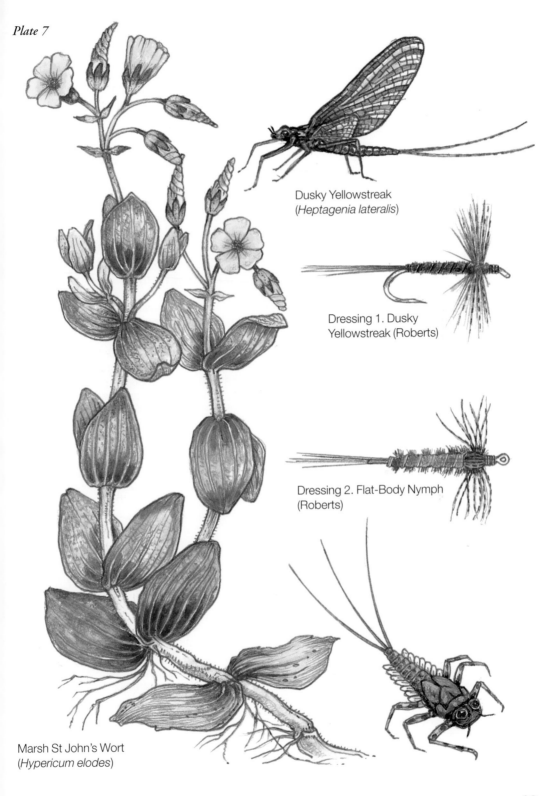

Dusky Yellowstreak
(*Heptagenia lateralis*)

Dressing 1. Dusky
Yellowstreak (Roberts)

Dressing 2. Flat-Body Nymph
(Roberts)

Marsh St John's Wort
(*Hypericum elodes*)

2. Flat-Body Nymph (Roberts)

DRESSING

Hook length: 12mm
Thread: Brown
Tail: Brown cock fibres
Abdomen: Brown ostrich herl
Rib: Gold wire
Thorax: Brown rabbit's fur
Wingcase: Brown cock fibres
Legs: Pale-brown partridge fibres

Marsh St John's Wort
Hypericum elodes (Plate 7)
St John's Wort family (*Guttiferae*)

Flower head:	Loose clusters of bell-shaped yellow flowers, 10–15mm across. Each flower is made up of 5 oval petals, many yellow stamens and 5 sepals with red margins. Flowers do not open widely
Leaves:	Oval to round in shape with many grey hairs on the under surface, growing in opposite pairs which half clasp the stem
Flowering time:	June–September
Height:	Up to 30cm
Habit:	Native perennial
Habitat:	Damp places, pond and stream margins in acid soil
Distribution:	Widespread but somewhat local. It is found mostly in western and southern areas of Britain
General:	*Hypericum* comes from the Greek *hyper* 'above', and *eikon* 'picture' – it was a plant hung above pictures to ward off evil spirits;

elodes refers to its habit of growing in marshy places. It is related to common St John's Wort, which in recent times has been found to be a useful remedy in curing depression

Iron Blue
Baetis niger, muticus (Plate 8)

The two species known as the Iron Blue are so similar they are regarded for fishing purposes and dressings as the same fly. It is a small fly that will put up with any sort of conditions: I have seen them hatching off in a snow storm with the fish rising to take them but they are just as accommodating in perfect condition. The main points of recognition are the small size and the overall dark colouration. Although mainly regarded as a very early and late season fly, the Iron Blue can be on the water throughout the fishing season.

Nymph:	
Size:	Up to 9mm
Colour:	Olive/dark green
Type:	Agile darter
Adult:	
Size:	Up to 7mm
Colour:	Dun: Female: dark olive-brown abdomen, grey-blue wings, olive-brown legs, olive eyes, blue-grey tails
	Male: abdomen as female, grey-blue wings, olive legs, dark red-brown eyes, blue-grey tails
	Spinner: Female: claret-brown abdomen, bright transparent wings, pale olive-grey legs,

red-brown eyes, pale olive-grey tails Male: translucent white abdomen, last three segments rich orange-brown, dark-brown thorax area, bright transparent wings, pale-grey legs, red-brown eyes, pale-grey tails

Habitat: Baetis muticus prefers stony streams and rivers. Baetis niger prefers weedy streams and rivers

Distribution: Common throughout Britain

Time of day: During the day

Time of year: Covers all the fishing season with early and late season main hatches

Shape of rear wing: Very small oval with coastal projection

Water Forget-Me-Not
Myosotis scorpioides (Plate 8)
Borage family (*Boraginaceae*)
(Water Mouse Ear, Scorpion Grass, Bird's Eye)

Flower head: Flowers 4–10mm across with pale blue petals, slightly notched at the top and with a yellow eye. The calyx teeth are triangular and about one third of the length of the calyx tube. The flowers are in loose clusters, the top of which is curved over rather like a shepherd's crook whilst ▶

Dressings

1. Iron Blue-dun (Warrilow)

DRESSING

Hook length: 7mm
Thread: Crimson
Tail: White cock fibres
Abdomen: Dark heron herl with a crimson tip
Wing: Shaped dark dun feathers
Hackle: Dark-dun cock

2. Iron Blue-dun

DRESSING

Hook length: 7mm
Thread: Crimson
Tail: Iron-blue cock fibres
Abdomen: Mole's fur
Wing: Grey poly yarn
Hackle: Iron-blue cock tied parachute

3. Iron Blue Nymph (Hidy)

DRESSING

Hook length: 10mm
Thread: Claret
Tail: Blue-dun fibres
Abdomen: Mole's fur
Thorax: Mole's fur
Legs: Dark blue-dun

4. Iron Blue Nymph (Skues)

DRESSING

Hook length: 9mm
Thread: Claret
Tail: White cock fibres
Abdomen: Claret tip then mole's fur
Thorax: Mole's fur
Wingcase: Black feather fibres
Legs: The tips of the wingcase fibres tied under

Plate 8

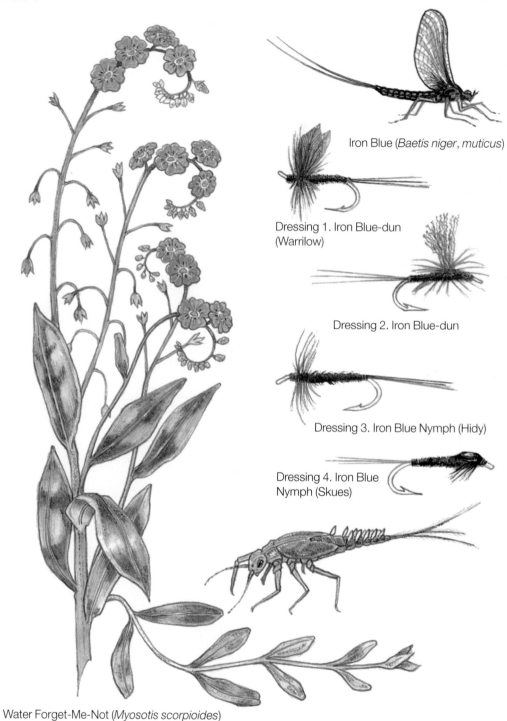

Iron Blue (*Baetis niger*, *muticus*)

Dressing 1. Iron Blue-dun (Warrilow)

Dressing 2. Iron Blue-dun

Dressing 3. Iron Blue Nymph (Hidy)

Dressing 4. Iron Blue Nymph (Skues)

Water Forget-Me-Not (*Myosotis scorpioides*)

▶ the flowers are in bud.
Flower colour may
occasionally be pink or
white

Leaves: Elongated and lance-
shaped leaves which feel
smooth to the touch – any
hairs they have are short
and lie flat along the
surface. Lower leaves are
stalked whilst the upper are
unstalked. All leaves are
alternate and have
untoothed margins

Fruit: A cluster of four shiny,
black nutlets within a calyx

Flowering time: May–September

Height: Up to 50cm

Habit: Perennial

Habitat: Rivers, streams and other
wet places

Distribution: Common throughout

General: This hairless or slightly
hairy perennial is the
commonest of the four
Forget-Me-Nots that grow
beside water. It is an erect
plant with creeping runners
and stems that sometimes
reach up to 140cm long.
Forget-Me-Nots are
traditionally associated
with true love and the
flower was often worn by a
person to ensure that a
sweetheart stayed faithful.
According to legend,
Forget-Me-Nots acquired
their name because Adam,
when naming the plants in
the Garden of Eden, totally
overlooked this tiny flower.
Another version, perhaps
more romantic, is that a
German knight, whilst
walking along a riverbank
with his lady, bent to collect
her a posy of flowers. He
overbalanced and fell into
the water and threw her the
posy, entreating her to
'forget him not'.
Botanically, the name is
derived from two Greek
words, *mus*, 'mouse', and
otos, 'ear' – mouse-ear – a
reference to the shape of
the leaves. *Scorpioides* is a
reference to the fact that
Water Forget-Me-Not was
believed to be effective
against the bite of a
scorpion because the
shape of the flower in bud
resembles a scorpion's tail
– hence, scorpion grass.
Medicinally, derivatives of
Forget-Me-Not were used
in the form of a syrup to
cure lung complaints

Lake Olive
Cloeon simile (Plate 9)

In general, the Lake Olive prefers larger and
deeper areas of water than its close relative,
Cloeon dipterum, the Pond Olive. The Lake
Olive is one of those flies that can vary in size
and colour but its normal appearance is
duller than the Pond Olive, and on closer
examination the tails are dark grey – the Pond
Olive's are light grey with brown rings. For
fishing purposes, the same patterns would do
for both flies. The larvae of the Lake Olive
seem to prefer the deeper, cooler water of
lakes, whilst the Pond Olive is chiefly found in
shallower ponds and lakes. Both species can
also be found in slow-flowing sections of
streams and rivers. They are also often the
only upwinged nymphs of any significance
present in some lowland still waters.

Nymph:
Size: Up to 12mm
Colour: Olive brown
Type: Agile darter

Adult:
Size: Up to 9mm
Colour: Dun: Female: medium red-brown abdomen with olive tinge and pale-olive segmentation, grey wings with a yellowish colouration to leading edge, olive-green legs, olive eyes with brown spot, dark-grey tails
Male: as female
Spinner: Female: red-brown abdomen tending to olive-brown under, bright wings with a tinge of yellow, olive legs, olive-green eyes, cream tails
Male: as female, but the abdomen is olive-brown with last three segments red-brown

Habitat: Larger ponds, lakes and slow sections of rivers
Distribution: Widely distributed throughout the British Isles
Time of day: Throughout the day
Time of year: Throughout the fishing season with early and late main hatches
Shape of rear wing: No rear wing

Dressings

1. Lake Olive Dun (Lapsley)

DRESSING

Hook length: 10mm
Thread: Brown
Tail: Light-dun cock fibres
Abdomen: Olive condor herl
Rib: Silver wire
Hackle: Medium blue-dun

2. Lake Olive (Masters)

DRESSING

Hook length: 10mm
Thread: Olive
Tail: Artist's paintbrush fibres
Abdomen: Extended light-olive antron
Rib: Silver wire
Wing: Cut from pale-green plastic bag
Hackle: Cul-de-canard

3. Lake Olive Nymph (Lane)

DRESSING

Hook length: 12mm
Thread: Golden olive
Tail: Olive cock fibres
Abdomen: Olive silk
Rib: Gold wire
Thorax: Olive silk
Legs: Olive cock fibres under

4. Lake Olive Nymph

DRESSING

Hook length: 12mm
Thread: Olive
Tail: Brown-olive fibres
Abdomen: Olive floss
Rib: Gold wire
Thorax: Hare's ear
Legs: Short olive cock

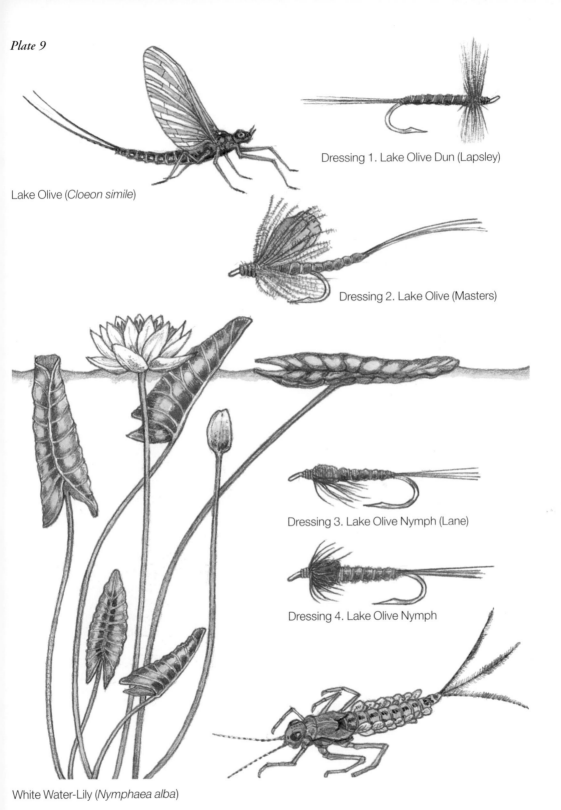

Plate 9

Dressing 1. Lake Olive Dun (Lapsley)

Lake Olive (*Cloeon simile*)

Dressing 2. Lake Olive (Masters)

Dressing 3. Lake Olive Nymph (Lane)

Dressing 4. Lake Olive Nymph

White Water-Lily (*Nymphaea alba*)

White Water-Lily
Nymphaea alba (**Plate 9**)
Water-Lily family (*Nymphaeaceae*)
(Lady of the Lake, Water Rose, Swan
Amongst the Flowers)

Flower head: White, many petalled
flowers, 10–20cm in
diameter. Four sepals,
which are green on the
outside, enclose upwards
of 20 white petals and
numerous yellow stamens
in an open fragrant flower
head

Leaves: Large, heart-shaped
floating leaves which are
carried at the end of long,
rope-like stems

Flowering time: July–August

Height: Up to 2m

Habit: Native perennial

Habitat: Lakes or ponds, in stagnant
or slow-flowing, warmish
water

Distribution: Common throughout

General: It is from the White Water-
Lily, crossed with exotic
species, that many of the
species of cultivated water
lilies of the modern times
have appeared. The name
Nymphaea alba comes
from Greek *nymphe*, water
nymph, and *alba*, meaning
'white'. In Elizabethan times
the seeds, made into a
broth, were said to cool
passions and the flower
was seen as representing
absolute purity. The leaves,
if well cooked, were once
eaten as a vegetable, whilst
the fresh root could be used
as a soap substitute. Other
uses were as a gargle for
sore throats, and externally
as a cure for ulcers

Large Brook Dun
Ecdyonorus torrentis (**Plate 10**)

The Large Brook Dun, as its name implies,
is a fly of the faster, stony rivers and streams.
It is another fly that, like the Late March
Brown, was once confused with the March
Brown, size and colouration both being
similar. Because of this, March Brown
patterns are used to imitate this species. The
nymph is a stone-clinger and prefers to crawl
out of the water to hatch the dun therefore is
mostly available to the trout on windy days,
when it is blown onto the water. The spinner,
like the dun, shares its name with that of the
two similar flies and is referred to as the Large
Red Spinner. Both male and female spinners
can become available to trout when
swarming takes place over the waterside
margins.

Nymph:

Size: Up to 15mm

Colour: Fawn-brown with darker
markings

Type: Stone-clinger

Adult:

Size: Up to 13mm

Colour: Dun: Female: olive-brown
abdomen with red-brown
colouration to sides looking
like diagonal banding, mottled
ginger-fawn wings with dark-
brown veins giving the
appearance of darker bands,
olive-brown legs, dark-brown
eyes, red-brown tails
Male: as female, but with
brown-black eyes and dark-
brown tails
Spinner: Female: red-brown
abdomen with darker diagonal
bands, bright transparent
wings with brown veins, olive
to red-brown legs, red-brown
eyes, red-brown tails
Male: as female but with

Plate 10

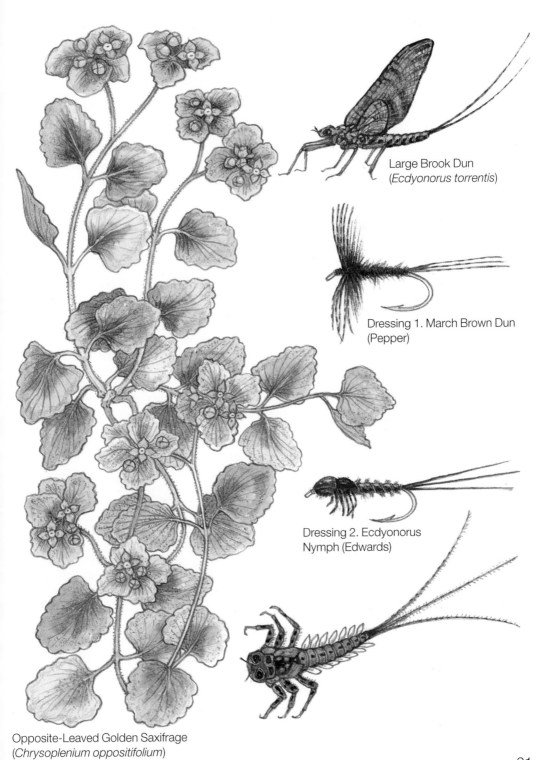

Large Brook Dun
(*Ecdyonorus torrentis*)

Dressing 1. March Brown Dun
(Pepper)

Dressing 2. Ecdyonorus
Nymph (Edwards)

Opposite-Leaved Golden Saxifrage
(*Chrysoplenium oppositifolium*)

darker, longer tails and brown-black eyes

Habitat: Fast, stony rivers and streams
Distribution: Uncommon but spread through most of Britain
Time of day: Throughout the day
Time of year: April–July
Shape of rear wing: Upright with coastal projection

Dressings

1. March Brown Dun (Pepper)

DRESSING

Hook length: 12mm
Thread: Purple
Tail: Brown partridge
Abdomen: Hare's ear
Hackle: Brown partridge with honey cock

2. Ecdyonorus Nymph (Edwards)

DRESSING

Hook length: Up to 15mm
Thread: Brown
Tail: Spaced moose mane hairs
Abdomen: Under copper wire to shape and flattened covered with yellow olive-brown fur
Rib: Gold wire
Thorax: As abdomen
Wingcase: Cock pheasant fibres
Head: As abdomen but coated with varnish and brown raffene over
Legs: Brown partridge cut to length

Opposite-Leaved Golden Saxifrage
Chrysoplenium oppositifolium (Plate 10)
Saxifrage family (*Saxifragaceae*)

Flower head: Small yellow flowers, 2–3mm across, consisting of 4 sepals and 4 stamens but not petals. The flowers are carried in flat clusters on upright stems
Leaves: Round in shape with bluntly toothed margins. The leaves are carried in opposite pairs on short, creeping stems which form a dense, flat turf
Flowering time: April–July
Height: Up to 10cm
Habit: Native perennial
Habitat: Stream sides and damp places
Distribution: Widespread, locally common except in eastern counties
General: This mat-forming perennial is found growing in places with acid or calcium-deficient soils. It is pollinated either by wind or by the tiny flies that are found near water. *Chrysoplenium* comes from the Greek *chrysos*, meaning 'gold', and '*splen*', meaning 'spleen'

Large Dark Olive
Baetis rhodani (Plate 11)

The Large Dark Olive, although not a particularly large fly, is larger than most other olives and the commonest species in the genus. It is also one of the most accommodating flies for fishing purposes as it is not only one of the first flies to put in an appearance in the fishing year, but it has also adapted to a very wide range of water conditions and locations. It can be found from April onwards, and hatches in sufficient numbers to cause interest from the trout. As it is such an early season fly it can also prove of great interest to the grayling. Although the main hatches are around March and April and then again, on a smaller scale, in autumn, the Large Dark Olive can be found on mild days all through the winter months. It inhabits not only alkaline chalk streams but also more acid, stony rivers and streams. A similar fly, the Dark Olive Dun, *Baetis atrebatinus*, which also hatches mostly in the early and late parts of the season, can be distinguished from the Large Dark Olive by its slightly smaller size and the lack of the small coastal projection on the hindwing.

Nymph:
Size: Up to 12mm
Colour: Pale to dark green
Type: Agile darter

Adult:
Size: Up to 10mm
Colour: Dun: Female: olive-brown abdomen, pale olive-grey wings, olive legs, olive-brown eyes, olive-grey tails
Male: as female, but with orange-brown eyes
Spinner: Female: red-brown abdomen with paler segmentation, bright transparent wings with pale-brown veins, olive legs, red-brown eyes, pale-brown tails
Male: as female, but with olive-brown abdomen
Habitat: From fast rivers to chalk streams
Distribution: Common and throughout most of Britain
Time of day: Throughout the day
Time of year: Any time of year but particularly April, May, September, October
Shape of rear wing: Small and oval with small coastal projection

Dressings

1. The Imperial (Kite)

DRESSING

Hook length: 10mm
Thread: Purple
Tail: Grey hackle fibres
Abdomen: Heron herl
Rib: Gold wire
Hackle: Honey-dun cock

2. Large Dark Olive Nymph (Price)

DRESSING

Hook length: 12mm
Thread: Yellow
Tail: Olive hackle fibres
Abdomen: Olive seal's fur sub mixed with hare's ear
Rib: Gold wire
Thorax: Brown seal's fur sub mixed with hare's ear and picked out
Wingcase: Olive goose fibres
Legs: Wingcase fibres turned under

Plate 11

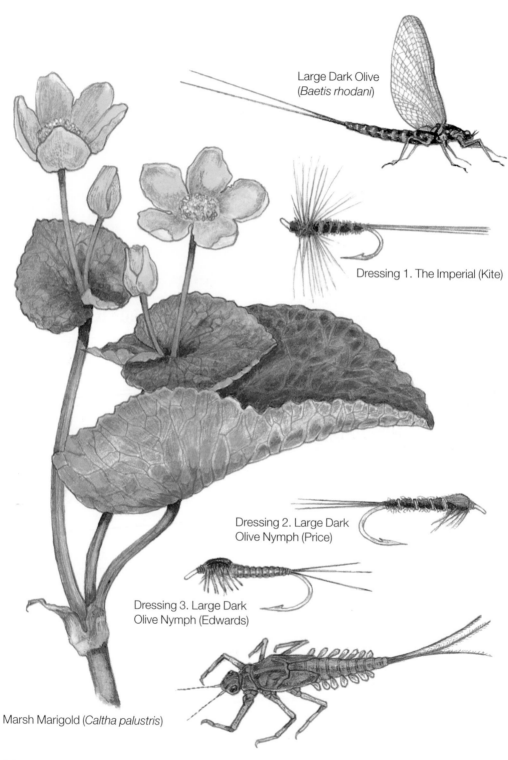

Large Dark Olive
(*Baetis rhodani*)

Dressing 1. The Imperial (Kite)

Dressing 2. Large Dark
Olive Nymph (Price)

Dressing 3. Large Dark
Olive Nymph (Edwards)

Marsh Marigold (*Caltha palustris*)

3. Large Dark Olive Nymph (Edwards)

DRESSING

Hook length: 12mm
Thread: White
Tail: Badger hair dyed olive
Abdomen: Olive flexibody
Thorax: Olive-brown hare's fur
Wingcase: Turkey feather fibres on each side leaving strip of olive flexibody down the centre
Legs: Olive-dyed partridge feather

Marsh Marigold
Caltha palustris (Plate 11)
Buttercup family (*Ranunculaceae*)
(Kingcup, Mollyblobs, Meadowbright, Mayblob)

Flower head:	Glossy, large yellow buttercup-like flower up to 5cm in diameter. The 5–8 oval 'petals' form saucer-shaped flower heads that are carried in loosely branched clusters on hollow stems
Leaves:	The glossy, kidney-shaped leaves with finely toothed edges are often mottled. Lower leaves are held on long, grooved stalks whilst those higher up the plant have very little, if any, stalk
Flowering time:	March–July
Height:	Up to 60cm
Habit:	Native perennial
Habitat:	Wet woods and meadows, river banks, streams and ditches
Distribution:	Common throughout
General:	This native perennial likes deep mud that is rich in soil nutrients. Its foliage, which when crushed gives off a sweet, sickly smell, contains poisons that cause colic and dysentery to cattle if eaten fresh. These poisons are removed if the foliage is dried. The name comes from the Latin *caltha*, meaning 'a plant with a yellow flower', and *palustris*, meaning 'marsh'. The commonest English name, 'Kingcup', is derived from the old English word 'cop' which meant 'button'. In France the plant is referred to as *bouton d'or* or 'golden button'. In May Marsh Marigold was frequently hung in doorways in order to ward off evil and to give some protection against lightning

Large Green Dun
Ecdyonurus insignis (Plate 12)

This is a fairly uncommon fly with a limited distribution. Furthermore the nymph, which is a stone-clinger, generally crawls out of the water to hatch so allowing the limited number of duns to escape the clutches of the trout. Because of these reasons it is of limited use to the fly fisherman.

Nymph:	
Size:	Up to 15mm
Colour:	Olive to dark brown
Type:	Stone-clinger
Adult:	
Size:	Up to 13mm
Colour:	Dun: Female: olive-brown-green abdomen, fawn-brown

wings well marked with a ginger shade to the leading edge and with a clear central area where just the main veins show, olive legs, dark brown eyes, dark olive-brown tails
Male: orange-brown abdomen, wings as female, pale-brown legs, dark red-brown eyes, dark-brown tails
Spinner: Female: orange-brown abdomen with darker segmentation, transparent wings with darker patches along the outer leading edge, orange-brown legs, dark-brown tails
Male: more olive-brown with very long tails up to 3 times the body length

Habitat: Found chiefly in stony rivers
Distribution: Uncommon, southern Wales, northern England and the West Country
Time of day: Throughout the day
Time of year: May–October, main hatches around July–August
Shape of rear wing: Large with coastal projections

Dressings

1. Large Green Dun (Veniard)

DRESSING

Hook length: 13mm
Thread: Brown
Tail: Dun cock fibres
Abdomen: A mix of green and grey seal's fur sub
Rib: Brown tying thread
Hackle: Cock hackle dyed green with a dyed green grizzle in front

2. Emerger Nymph (Jardine)

DRESSING

Hook length: Up to 15mm
Thread: Brown
Tail: Lemon wood duck
Abdomen: Olive-brown fur
Rib: Brown thread
Thorax: Antron fur loop over
Wing: Lemon wood duck

3. Ecdyonorus Nymph (Edwards)

DRESSING

Hook length: Up to 15mm
Thread: Brown
Tail: Three hairs from moose mane
Abdomen: Olive fur dubbed and picked out through rib
Rib: Gold wire
Thorax: As abdomen
Wingcase: Cock pheasant fibres
Head: As abdomen but coated with varnish and brown raffene over
Legs: Partridge cut to length

Indian Balsam
Impatiens glandulifera (Plate 12)

Balsam family (*Balsaminaceae*) (Himalayan Balsam, Policeman's Helmet, Touch-Me-Not)

Flower head: Pink, red, purple, mauve or white flowers 2.5–4cm long with a short, downward-pointing spur. Each flower is made up of one large helmet-shaped upper petal and two ▶

Plate 12

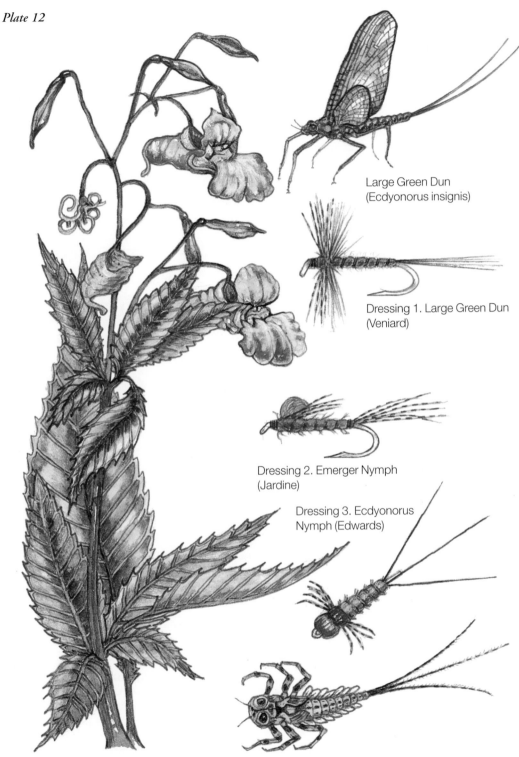

Large Green Dun
(Ecdyonorus insignis)

Dressing 1. Large Green Dun
(Veniard)

Dressing 2. Emerger Nymph
(Jardine)

Dressing 3. Ecdyonorus
Nymph (Edwards)

Indian Balsam (*Impatiens glandulifera*)

▶ smaller lower petals which form a lip and are often spotted in the throat. They are held in erect clusters of between 5 and 20 flowers

Leaves: Lance-shaped leaves, 10–25cm long, dark green in colour and with red stems. They appear in opposite pairs in 3–5 whorls and have sharply serrated margins

Flowering time: July–October

Height: Up to 3m

Habit: Introduced annual

Habitat: Waste places, muddy areas, banks of rivers and lakes, ditches

Distribution: Naturalized throughout region – locally abundant in England and Wales but rarer elsewhere

General: This hairless, robust plant was introduced as a garden plant in 1840 from the Himalayas but soon appeared in the wild, where it spread widely, colonizing wet places. The Latin *impatiens*, meaning 'impatient', is a reference to its highly effective method of spreading seed. The capsules that enclose the seed need only the slightest touch to cause them to burst open and shoot the seeds out explosively, spreading them a good distance from the parent plant. The flowers are extremely attractive to bumble bees, which act as pollinators for them. When a bee visits the plant to collect nectar it crawls inside the flower and is completely enclosed by it. Pollen is then deposited from the bee's body onto the stigma whilst, at the same time, more pollen rubs off onto the bee's body from the male stamens. When the bee flies off to visit another flower some of this pollen will be deposited onto the next flower and so ensure cross-pollination. Both flowers and foliage have a sickly-sweet smell when crushed

Large Spurwing
Centroptilum pennulatum
(Plate 13)

When at rest, most of the upwinged flies hold their wings close together, but the Large Spurwing has the habit of resting with the wings held apart. As the name implies, the small hindwings have a coastal projection or spur. The fly has a preference for sandy, weedy bottoms on slow-flowing sections of streams and rivers. A point of identification between the Large Spurwing and the Small Spurwing, apart from its size, is the rounded apex to the hindwing – in the Small Spurwing the apex is pointed. This is, of course, only discernible with some form of magnifying lens. Hatches are usually sparse but when coming off the water with other flies it is said the trout will prefer the Large Spurwing, so at these times a reasonably accurate copy is called for.

Nymph:
Size: Up to 10mm
Colour: Buff with darker markings
Type: Agile darter

Adult:
Size: Up to 9mm
Colour: Dun: Female: pale-olive ▶

Plate 13

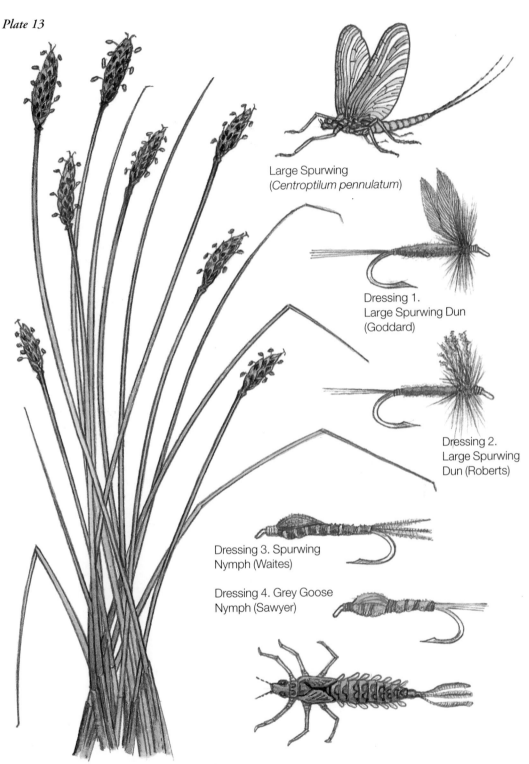

Large Spurwing
(*Centroptilum pennulatum*)

Dressing 1.
Large Spurwing Dun
(Goddard)

Dressing 2.
Large Spurwing
Dun (Roberts)

Dressing 3. Spurwing
Nymph (Waites)

Dressing 4. Grey Goose
Nymph (Sawyer)

Common Spike Rush (*Eleocharis palustris*)

▶ abdomen, smoke-grey wings, olive legs, olive eyes, olive-grey tails
Male: brown-olive abdomen with last three segments orange-brown, smoke-grey wings, olive legs, orange eyes, olive-grey tails
Spinner: Female: amber abdomen with pale-amber segmentation, bright transparent wings, olive legs, pale-olive eyes, light-grey tails
Male: grey-white abdomen with last three segments orange-brown, transparent wings, olive legs, orange eyes, light-grey tails

Habitat: Weeds in slow stretches of rivers and streams preferably with sandy bottoms
Distribution: Uncommon but found throughout Britain
Time of day: Throughout the day
Time of year: May–October
Shape of rear wing: Small oval with rounded apex and coastal projection 'spur'

Dressings

1. Large Spurwing Dun (Goddard)

DRESSING

Hook length: 10mm
Thread: Cream
Tail: Blue-dun hackle fibres
Abdomen: Cream seal's fur
Wing: Pale starling tied with a definite V-shape
Hackle: Olive cock

2. Large Spurwing Dun (Roberts)

DRESSING

Hook length: 10mm
Thread: Cream
Tail: Cream cock fibres
Abdomen: Olive-grey seal's fur sub
Wing: Blue-grey poly yarn
Hackle: Pale olive

3. Spurwing Nymph (Waites)

DRESSING

Hook length: 10mm
Thread: Grey
Tail: Heron herl tips
Abdomen: Natural heron herl
Rib: Silver fuse-wire
Wingcase: Heron herl over thorax area

4. Grey Goose Nymph (Sawyer)

DRESSING

Hook length: 10mm
Thread: None
Tail: Grey goose fibres
Abdomen: Grey goose fibres and copper wire wound onto an underbody of copper wire
Thorax: As abdomen, built up with grey goose fibres doubled over the top

Common Spike Rush
Eleocharis palustris (Plate 13)
Sedge family (*Cyperaceae*)

Flower head:	Bisexual flowers in a spike on erect, hairless, slightly flattened stems which are reddish at the base. Yellowish to dark-brown flowers have 3 stamens and 2 stigmas enclosed by a bract and are in spikes of 3–20mm in length
Leaves:	Leafless plant
Flowering time:	May–July
Height:	Up to 60cm
Habit:	Perennial
Habitat:	Ponds, riverbanks, marshes and wet meadows
Distribution:	Common throughout
General:	Closely related to members of the sedge family and leafless like other members of the rush species, this creeping plant is abundant and widespread where it grows. Its name is derived from Greek *helodes* – 'growing in marshes' – and *charis*, meaning 'grace'

Large Summer Dun
Siphlonorus lacustris (*alternatus, armatus*) (Plate 14)

Of the three species, *lacustris* is the only one of particular interest to the fly fisherman. All three species are found in similar habitats, chiefly slow-flowing sections of rivers and streams, lakes and areas of water at altitude, Scottish and some Irish lochs. Emergence of all three species is said to take place partly or entirely out of the water on some convenient plant or rock. As with all species that develop by this method, the dun is therefore barely available to the trout except as windborne casualties, and so on. The fly itself is very distinctive, being little smaller than the Mayfly with an overall rich olive-brown colouration. The nymph is large, up to 18mm long, and belongs to the group known as the agile darters. The gills are pronounced and consist of double and single plates.

Nymph:	
Size:	Up to 18mm
Colour:	Olive-brown
Type:	Agile darter
Adult:	
Size:	Up to 15mm
Colour:	Dun: Female: dark-olive abdomen, grey-olive wings, olive-brown legs, dark-brown eyes, dark olive-brown tails Male: as female. Spinner: Female: green-brown abdomen, transparent wings with pale-brown veins, dark-olive legs, red-brown eyes, dark-olive tails Male: as female
Habitat:	Slow-flowing sections of rivers and streams, lakes and Scottish and Irish lochs
Distribution:	Fairly rare but found locally throughout Britain and the limestone loughs of Ireland
Time of day:	Throughout the day
Time of year:	May–August
Shape of rear wing:	Large hindwings with coastal projection

Plate 14

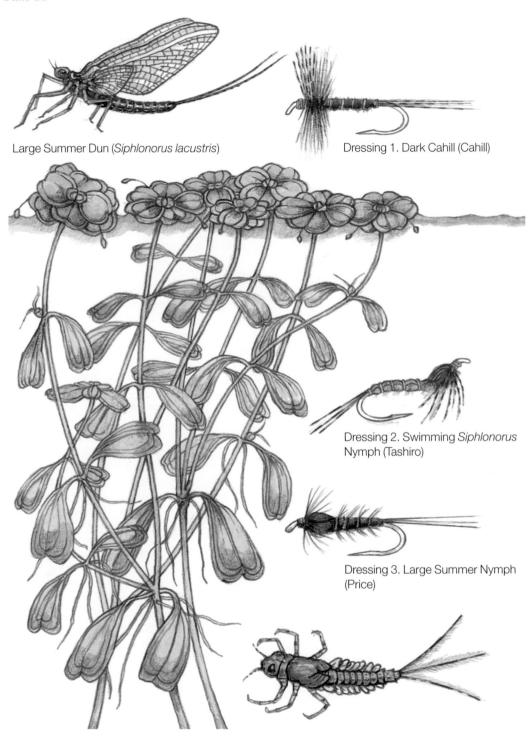

Large Summer Dun (*Siphlonorus lacustris*)

Dressing 1. Dark Cahill (Cahill)

Dressing 2. Swimming *Siphlonorus* Nymph (Tashiro)

Dressing 3. Large Summer Nymph (Price)

Water Starwort (*Callitriche stagnalis*)

Dressings

1. Dark Cahill (Cahill)

DRESSING

Hook length: Up to 14mm
Thread: Olive
Tail: Mandarin duck breast fibres
Abdomen: Olive-brown fur
Rib: Gold wire
Wing: Mandarin duck fibres
Hackle: Brown cock

2. Swimming *Siphlonorus* Nymph (Tashiro)

DRESSING

Hook length: Up to 18mm (bent at point of thorax)
Thread: Olive
Tail: Lady Amherst's pheasant tippet fibres
Abdomen: Olive-brown dubbing with barred wood duck fibres over
Rib: Round gold wire or tinsel
Thorax: As abdomen but with olive quill over
Legs: Brown partridge hackle

3. Large Summer Dun Nymph (Price)

DRESSING

Hook length: Up to 18mm
Thread: Brown
Tail: Olive-brown feather fibres
Abdomen: Olive-brown seal's fur sub with palmered olive hackle
Rib: Gold wire
Thorax: As abdomen
Wingcase: Brown feather fibres
Legs: Dark-olive cock hackle

Water Starwort
Callitriche stagnalis (Plate 14)
Starwort family (*Callitrichaceae*)

Flower head:	Tiny, inconspicuous green flowers appearing singly at the base of leaves. Flowers are four-lobed and have one pale yellow stamen
Leaves:	Up to 2cm long and in opposite pairs, bright green in colour. Submerged leaves are narrow and less round, upper leaves are short-stalked, more rounded and float in a rosette formation
Flowering time:	May–September
Height:	Up to 100cm
Habit:	Perennial
Habitat:	Slow-flowing waters, stagnant ponds, ditches and streams
Distribution:	Common
General:	Common Water Starwort is a plant that can vary in appearance according to its habitat. The shape of the leaves may be affected by the flow and depth of the water in which it is living. If growing in mud, the plant may only be a few centimetres high and look different from plants growing in water. *Callitriche* is taken from Greek and means 'beautiful hair' – a reference to the hair-like growth of roots and stems when growing in deep water; *stagnalis* refers to its liking for stagnant or still water

Late March Brown
Ecdyonorus venosus (Plate 15)

This fly is so similar to the March Brown that the species were for a long time thought to be one and the same. It is now realized that of the two the Late or False March Brown is the commoner and more widely distributed species. It is not only the size and colouration that causes the confusion, both being very similar, but the fact that both flies are found in the same locations, preferring fast-flowing, stony rivers and streams. One difference between the two is that the March Brown is an early season fly, March–April, but the Late March Brown, as the name suggests, has a season stretching into August–September. Overall, however, the flies are so similar that the same patterns will do for either. The nymph is another species that crawls out of the water onto stones to emerge so giving the trout little opportunity to take the duns in any numbers.

Nymph:
Size: Up to 15mm
Colour: Olive-brown to grey-brown with darker areas
Type: Stone-clinger

Adult:
Size: Up to 13mm
Colour: Dun: Female: dull-brown abdomen, grey-fawn-brown wings with dark veins giving a mottled effect, pale-brown legs, grey-brown tails
Male: as female but overall darker in appearance
Spinner: Female: rich red-brown abdomen, transparent wings with pale-brown veins, brown tails
Male is of no interest
Habitat: Stony streams and rivers
Distribution: Localized throughout Britain and Ireland
Time of day: Throughout the day
Time of year: May–October with the main hatches August–September
Shape of rear wing: Large with coastal projection

Dressings

1. March Brown Dun (Price)

DRESSING

Hook length: 13mm
Thread: Primrose
Tail: Cree hackle fibres
Abdomen: Hare's ear and yellow seal's fur sub
Rib: Primrose thread
Wing: Hen-pheasant slips
Hackle: Cree cock

2. March Brown Spider (Woolley)

DRESSING

Hook length: Up to 15mm
Thread: Orange
Tail: Speckled partridge
Abdomen: Sandy fur
Rib: Yellow thread
Wing: Speckled partridge
Hackle: Pale partridge

Plate 15

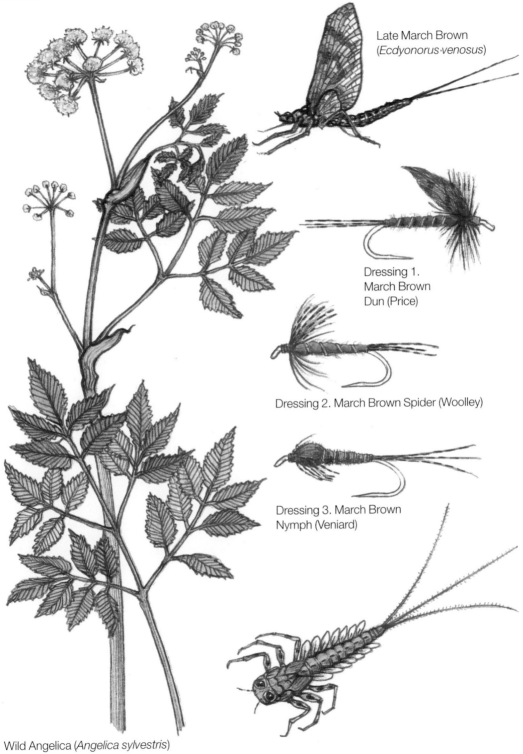

Late March Brown
(*Ecdyonorus·venosus*)

Dressing 1.
March Brown
Dun (Price)

Dressing 2. March Brown Spider (Woolley)

Dressing 3. March Brown
Nymph (Veniard)

Wild Angelica (*Angelica sylvestris*)

3. March Brown Nymph (Veniard)

DRESSING

Hook length: Up to 15mm
Thread: Brown
Tail: Brown mallard shoulder fibres or pheasant tail
Abdomen: Cock pheasant tail
Rib: Gold wire
Thorax: Hare's ear fur
Wingcase: Feather fibres from a woodcock wing
Legs: Speckled partridge

Wild Angelica
Angelica sylvestris (Plate 15)
Carrot family (*Umbelliferae*)

Flower head:	Umbrella-shaped flowerheads 5–15cm across and situated at the end of stalks coming from the angle between leaf and stem. The white or pinkish flowers have inwardly curving petals and no sepals
Leaves:	Large divided leaves on stalks up to 60cm long. Stalks are roughly triangular in shape and where they join the main stem form large swollen sheaths
Flowering time:	July–September
Height:	Up to 2m
Habit:	Native perennial
Habitat:	Fens, marshes, river and stream banks, wet areas
Distribution:	Common
General:	Usually a stout, almost hairless plant, Angelica is

another species which may vary in appearance according to its habitat – in places it grows to no more than 30cm tall. It has been a popular medicinal plant as its name, angelica or angelic, suggests, with both seeds and root being extremely useful in curing ailments. A close relative, *Angelica archangelica*, is eaten as a sweet and used in a crystallized form to decorate cakes and other foodstuffs

March Brown
Rhithrogena germanica (Plate 16)

Two species were originally known collectively as the March Brown – *Rhithrogena germanica* and *Ecdyonorus venosus* (the Late or False March Brown). Because of this confusion the March Brown was thought to be more commonly and widely distributed than it is and with a longer hatching period. However, it is now known that *Rhithrogena germanica* is a lot more localized and 'on the wing' over a much shorter period than at first thought. Because of this misunderstanding a greater number of patterns than would normally have been expected have been designed to imitate the 'March Brown'. The earlier hatches are now more than likely to be of *germanica*, and the hatches later in the year to be *Ecdyonorus venosus*. This goes to illustrate some of the problems with positive upwinged fly identification.

Nymph:	
Size:	Up to 15mm
Colour:	Olive brown
Type:	Stone-clinger

Adult:
Size: Up to 14mm
Colour: Dun: Female: rich dark-brown abdomen with pale-yellow banding, pale yellow-brown wings with dark-brown veins (but the middle of the wing has no veins and shows up as a distinctive clear area), dark-green eyes, dark-brown tails
Male: as female
Spinner: Female: rich red-brown abdomen with pale-yellow banding, transparent wings with brown veins, red-brown legs, dark-green eyes, mid-brown tails
Male: as female
Habitat: Fast flowing rivers
Distribution: Localized in parts of Scotland, Wales and northern England
Time of day: After midday
Time of year: March–April
Shape of rear wing: Large, upright with coastal projection

Dressings

1. March Brown (Courtney Williams)

DRESSING

Hook length: 14mm
Thread: Brown
Tail: Brown feather fibres
Abdomen: Grey-brown underfur from the hare
Wing: Hen pheasant feathers
Hackle: Brown cock

2. March Brown Floating Nymph (Jardine)

DRESSING

Hook length: 14mm
Thread: Brown
Tail: Lemon wood duck
Abdomen: Hare's fur
Thorax: Hare's fur with antron fur over
Wing: Lemon wood duck

3. March Brown Nymph (Roberts)

DRESSING

Hook length: 14mm
Thread: Brown
Tail: Three cock pheasant tail fibres
Abdomen: Cock pheasant tail fibres
Rib: Gold wire
Thorax: Hare's ear fur
Wingcase: Woodcock feather fibres doubled over thorax area
Legs: Brown partridge

Brooklime
Veronica beccabunga (Plate 16)
Figwort family (*Scrophulariaceae*)
(Water Pimpernel, Mouth Smart)

Flower head: Pale or dark blue flowers, 5–8mm across, carried on loose spikes growing from the angles of the stem and upper leaves. Each flower has four petal lobes – the upper being the largest – and two stamens
Leaves: Carried in pairs on short stalks, the leaves are oval

Plate 16

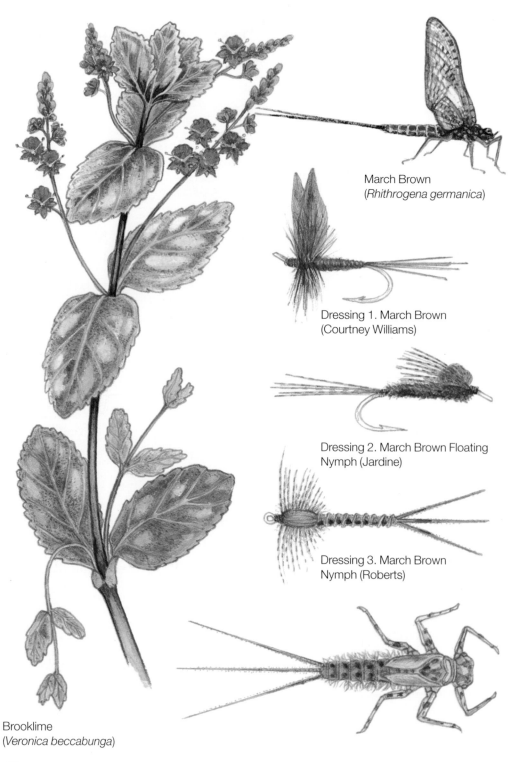

March Brown
(*Rhithrogena germanica*)

Dressing 1. March Brown
(Courtney Williams)

Dressing 2. March Brown Floating
Nymph (Jardine)

Dressing 3. March Brown
Nymph (Roberts)

Brooklime
(*Veronica beccabunga*)

to round in shape with a glossy, slightly fleshy appearance and blunt-toothed leaf margins

Fruit: Flattened, rounded capsule, slightly notched at the top

Flowering time: May–August

Height: Up to 60cm

Habit: Perennial

Habitat: Small streams and watery places, rivers and wet grasslands

Distribution: Common throughout, except northwest Scotland

General: This native perennial herb is one of a large family of *Veronica* species, many of which are familiar and all being very similar in appearance. It is a creeping, fleshy plant which takes root in the bottom mud, leaving its upper part floating in the water in a similar manner to watercress, with which it is often found growing. The hollow stems contain air spaces which allow the floating parts of the plant to absorb oxygen and transfer it down to the roots, which rely on oxygen for growth. The name *beccabunga* is probably derived from the Germanic word 'beck' meaning a stream, whilst 'lime' comes from the Latin *limus*, meaning 'mud'. In the seventeenth century drinks made from Brooklime were used as a cure for scurvy and to purge the blood. Its leaves fried in butter and vinegar and applied warm to tumours and inflammation were said to relieve the swelling. In modern usage it is believed to assist in the relief of migraines, indigestion, anorexia and fevers, and its leaves, although having a somewhat bitter taste, may be used as an addition to salads

Mayfly

Ephemera danica, vulgata, lineata (Plate 17)

Of the three species, *danica* is the most common, while *lineata* is so rare it can be discounted for fishing purposes. *Danica* and *vulgata* are very similar, the main difference being the abdominal markings, so from the fisherman's point of view they can be regarded as the same. The nymph of *danica* is found chiefly in lakes, streams and rivers with a sand or gravel bottom, while *vulgata* prefers rivers and lakes with a muddy bottom.

The Mayfly, for obvious reasons of size and colour, is by far the easiest to identify and the best known of all the fisherman's flies. It has been held in such high esteem by generations of fishermen that a part of the fishing calendar is given over to it, 'Mayfly Fortnight', or as it is sometimes denigrated to, 'Duffers Fortnight' (the latter term referring to the idea that all fishing is easy within the short Mayfly season – which of course it is not). There are days of easy fishing when the trout are feeding avidly on almost anything that comes over their heads, but you can also get days of extreme frustration. Easy fishing or difficult, the joy of watching these most beautiful of flies dancing and egg-laying over the water surface is sufficient reason to be on the river at this time of year.

The Mayfly nymph is the only burrowing nymph in Britain that makes tunnels in river

49

and lake beds with its especially adapted mandibles and gills. The nymph takes up to two years to mature and for the most of this time is unavailable to the trout. They only become available during their swim to the surface to hatch into the adult fly. The main hatch period is very short – from mid-May to mid-June – but can be very heavy, with flies littering the river causing a feeding frenzy amongst the trout. Although by far the greatest numbers of flies hatch at this time, odd stragglers can be found coming off the water as late as September, when they are of little interest to the fish.

Nymph:

Size:	Up to 25mm
Colour:	Cream with brown and sandy brown markings
Type:	Burrower

Adult:

Size:	Up to 20mm (large variations in size, and the male is often a lot smaller than the female)
Colour:	Dun: Female: creamy-yellow abdomen with brown markings, the wing-root thorax area often tinged red, creamy-yellow wings with obvious veins and small dark areas on main wings, creamy-brown legs, dark-brown eyes, grey-black tails Male: as female, but smaller Spinner: Female: creamy-white abdomen, last three segments with brown triangular markings, bright transparent wings with obvious veins and small dark areas, olive legs, olive-black eyes, dark-brown tails Male: as female, but smaller
Habitat:	*Danica* – faster flowing streams and rivers, also lakes with a sandy or gravel bottom.

Vulgata – slower flowing rivers and lakes with a muddy bottom

Distribution:	Widespread throughout Britain and Ireland
Time of day:	Mostly after midday
Time of year:	Mid-May–September but the main concentration is May–mid-June
Shape of rear wing:	Large with coastal projections

Dressings

1. Lively Mayfly (Lively)

DRESSING

Hook length: Up to 15mm (the body is extended beyond the hook)
Thread: Green
Tail: Three pheasant tail fibres
Abdomen: Extended in a curve upwards with deer hair fibres
Abdomen hackle: On hook length only a palmered grizzle
Rib: Green thread
Thorax: Creamy-yellow dubbing
Wings: Wood duck fibres in two bunches
Hackle: Golden-olive cock

2. Mayfly Emerger Nymph (Jardine)

DRESSING

Hook length: 20mm
Thread: Brown
Tail: Cock pheasant fibres
Abdomen: Cream rabbit's fur
Rib: Brown thread
Thorax: Dubbed brown fur
Wing buds: Dark brown
Emerging wing: Deer hair

Plate 17

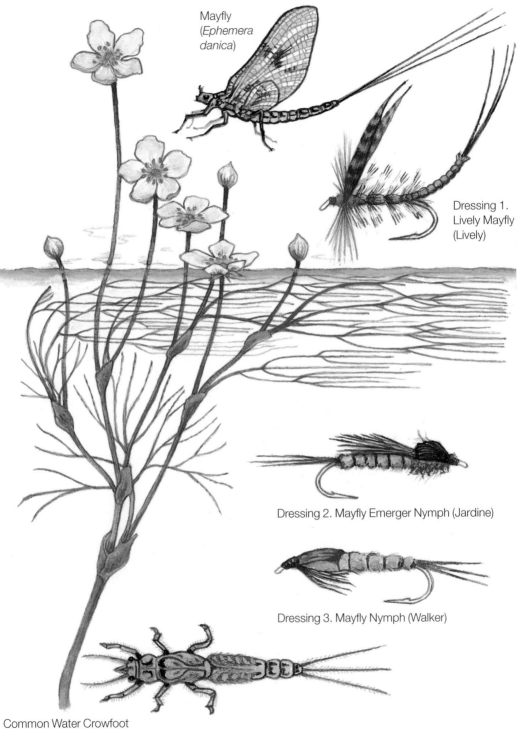

Mayfly
(*Ephemera danica*)

Dressing 1.
Lively Mayfly
(Lively)

Dressing 2. Mayfly Emerger Nymph (Jardine)

Dressing 3. Mayfly Nymph (Walker)

Common Water Crowfoot
(*Ranunculus aquatilis*)

3. Mayfly Nymph (Walker)

DRESSING

Hook length: 20mm
Thread: Brown
Tail: Pheasant tail fibres
Abdomen: Creamy angora wool
Rib: Pheasant tail and brown nylon thread in bands
Thorax: As abdomen
Wingcase: Pheasant tail fibres over thorax area ends tied under for legs

Common Water Crowfoot
Ranunculus aquatilis (Plate 17)
Buttercup family (*Ranunculaceae*)

Flower head:	Single, long-stalked, white and yellow flowers 1–3cm across, often floating in masses and held slightly above the water surface
Leaves:	Two types of leaf are present – floating and submerged. Floating leaves are broad and palmate whilst submerged leaves are finely divided into numerous short wisps
Flowering time:	May–June
Height:	Up to 120cm
Habit:	Perennial
Habitat:	Ponds, streams, ditches, stagnant or slow-moving water
Distribution:	Common, except Scotland
General:	Common Water Crowfoot is a plant that likes water rich in nutrients and seldom more than 1m deep. There are many other closely related species but this is the commonest in most areas. Like with other members of the buttercup family, the sap contains poisons

Medium Olive
Bateis vernus, tenax, buceratus (Plate 18)

Of the three species, *buceratus* is by far the rarest and can be discounted for fishing purposes. The other two species are so similar they are regarded as the same from the point of view of patterns, and there is some question as to whether they are a different species. The only distinction put forward is that *tenax* is mostly to be found in fast, stony streams in the mountains of Britain and so is more common in the north. *Vernus* prefers weedy, slow-flowing rivers in the south. On chalk streams hatches can be particularly heavy in May and June but lasting into September. The nymph swims to the surface to hatch and so the dun is readily available to the trout. By late afternoon the female spinner returns to the water looking for protruding objects that will assist her to crawl under the water to lay her eggs. On floating to the surface the spinner dies and once again becomes food for the trout.

Nymph:	
Size:	Up to 11mm
Colour:	Olive
Type:	Agile darter
Adult:	
Size:	Up to 9mm
Colour:	Dun: Female: olive-brown abdomen, paler underneath, grey wings tinged yellow-olive, yellow-olive legs, olive-green eyes, grey tails
	Male: as female, but abdomen is duller and the eyes are brown
	Spinner: Female: rich red-brown abdomen, bright transparent wings with pale-brown veins, grey-brown legs, brown eyes, pale-grey tails
	Male: grey-olive-brown

Plate 18

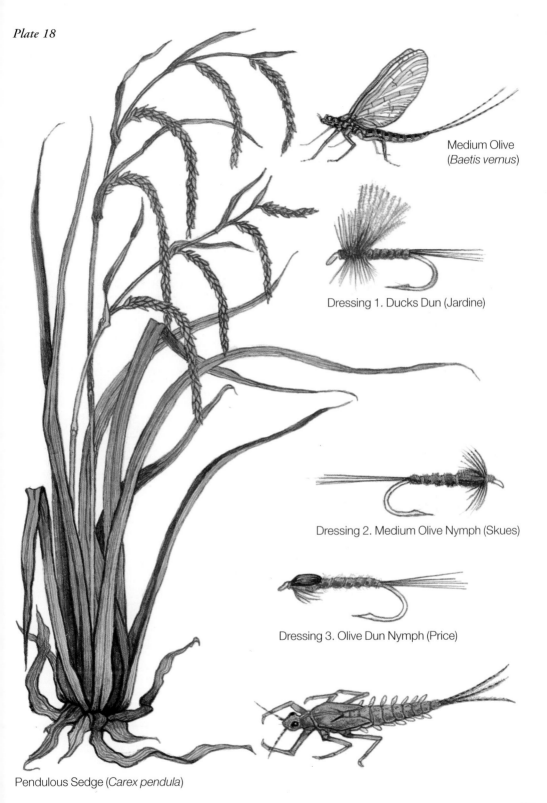

Medium Olive
(*Baetis vernus*)

Dressing 1. Ducks Dun (Jardine)

Dressing 2. Medium Olive Nymph (Skues)

Dressing 3. Olive Dun Nymph (Price)

Pendulous Sedge (*Carex pendula*)

abdomen with last three segments pale red-brown and contrasting darker thorax area, wings as female, grey-brown legs, brown eyes, pale-grey tails

Habitat: Slow-flowing sections of rivers with weed, and smaller stony upland streams

Distribution: Distributed widely throughout Britain

Time of day: Midday onwards

Time of year: April–October, the main hatch May–June

Shape of rear wing: Small oval with small coastal projection

Dressings

1. Ducks Dun (Jardine)

DRESSING

Hook length: 9mm
Thread: Hot orange
Tail: Fibres from spade hackle of jungle cock
Abdomen: Olive hairtran
Wings: Cul-de-canard
Hackle: Short-fibred blue-dun

2. Medium Olive Nymph (Skues)

DRESSING

Hook length: 11mm
Thread: Primrose
Tail: Pale-blue cock hackle fibres
Abdomen: Heron herl dyed olive
Rib: Gold wire
Thorax: Blue squirrel fur
Hackle: Dark-blue cock

3. Olive Dun Nymph (Price)

DRESSING

Hook length: 11mm
Thread: Olive
Tail: Olive hackle fibres
Abdomen: Olive seal's fur sub
Rib: Gold wire
Thorax: Olive seal's fur sub
Wingcase: Grey quill
Legs: Medium-olive hen

Pendulous Sedge
Carex pendula (Plate 18)
Sedge family (*Cyperaceae*)

Flower head: Reddish-brown spikes along the length of a triangular stem. A single male spike sits at the top with 4 or 5 female spikes lower down. Spikes are erect to begin with and then develop a drooping habit as they mature

Leaves: Broad leaves, about 2.5cm wide with a keel on the back and rough edges. Yellowish-green on top and bluish-green below, they form a sheath around the stem

Flowering time: May–June
Height: 1.5m
Habit: Perennial
Habitat: Riverbanks, damp woodlands
Distribution: Widespread, except in Scotland
General: The drooping flower spikes of this common sedge often look like catkins as they blow in the breeze. *Carex* is taken from the Greek *kairo* meaning 'to cut', and refers to the sharp, rough edges of the leaves

Olive Upright
Rhithrogena semicolorata
(Plate 19)

This is one of the more common upwinged flies and reasonably well distributed, although it is said to have a preference for the western areas of England. It is an important fly where it does occur and can, if weather conditions are suitable, hatch in large numbers after midday, causing a good evening rise. The overall appearance of the fly is similar to, if a little larger than, the Blue-Winged Olive, but the Olive Upright has only two tails, while the Blue-Winged Olive has three.

Nymph:
Size:	Up to 15mm
Colour:	Olive brown
Type:	Stone-clinger

Adult:
Size:	Up to 12mm
Colour:	Dun: Female: olive-brown abdomen ringed pale olive, dull orange thorax, blue-grey wings, pale-brown legs, dark-green eyes, pale-brown tails Male: abdomen and thorax as female, blue-grey wings, brown-black eyes, pale-brown tails Spinner: Female: pale olive-brown abdomen with paler banding, transparent wings with pale-brown veins, pale-olive legs, pale-olive eyes, pale olive-grey tails Male: as female
Habitat:	Stony, fast rivers
Distribution:	England, Wales and west Scotland
Time of day:	Afternoon–evening
Time of year:	April–July
Shape of rear wing:	Large, upright with coastal projection

Dressings

1. Olive Upright (Mawle)

DRESSING

Hook length: 12mm
Thread: Primrose
Tail: Grizzle fibres
Abdomen: Yellow, cream and olive seal's fur sub
Rib: Gold wire
Wing: Pale blue-dun hackle feathers
Hackle: Grizzle cock

2. Olive Suspender Nymph (Goddard)

DRESSING

Hook length: 15mm
Thread: Brown
Tail: Greenwell fibres
Abdomen: Olive goose feather fibres
Rib: Gold wire
Thorax: Olive feather fibres
Wingcase: Pheasant tail fibres or brown fibres over thorax area; a ball of ethafoam, enmeshed in nylon tights, is tied in and coloured grey
Legs: Tips of wingcase material tied under

3. Blue-Winged Olive Nymph (Edwards)

DRESSING

Hook length: 15mm
Thread: Orange
Tail: Partridge fibres
Abdomen: Sandy-brown hare's ear
Rib: Gold wire
Thorax: Sandy-brown hare's ear
Wingcase: Pheasant tail fibres tied either side of thorax area leaving a stripe of thorax colour showing on top
Legs: Partridge hackle each side of thorax only

Plate 19

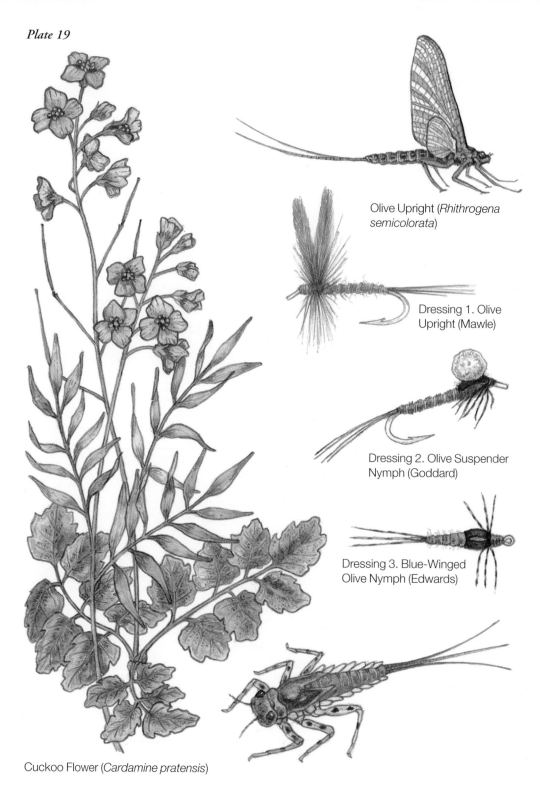

Olive Upright (*Rhithrogena semicolorata*)

Dressing 1. Olive Upright (Mawle)

Dressing 2. Olive Suspender Nymph (Goddard)

Dressing 3. Blue-Winged Olive Nymph (Edwards)

Cuckoo Flower (*Cardamine pratensis*)

Cuckoo Flower
Cardamine pratensis (Plate 19)
Mustard family (*Cruciferae*)
(Lady's Smock, Milkmaid, Lady's Mantle)

Flower head: The flowers, which are up to 20mm across, are gathered in small, loose clusters at the end of hollow, hairless and erect stems. Each consists of 4 broad, overlapping petals, short narrow sepals and a number of yellow anthers. Flower colour ranges from deep lilac to pink and very rarely white, depending on the habitat in which it is growing

Leaves: Dark green in colour with the basal leaves forming a rosette around the stem. These lower leaves are divided into between 7 and 10 pairs of rounded, slightly toothed leaflets, the terminal leaflet usually being the larger. Higher up the stem the leaflets become longer and narrower

Fruit: 2.5–4cm long, narrow rounded pods

Flowering time: April–June

Height: Up to 60cm

Habit: Perennial

Habitat: Moist meadows and streams

Distribution: Common throughout

General: This native perennial, one of the first flowers to appear in spring, is an indicator of rich ground and the presence of ground water. In appearance it resembles members of the cress family and its leaves can, in fact, be used as a substitute for watercress in salads – 'Bittercress' is one of its English names. Its most common name, 'Cuckoo Flower', is probably derived from the fact that it flowers mainly at around the same time as the cuckoo is heard singing. Alternatively, it is a plant often seen covered in a frothy, white substance that used to be thought of as 'cuckoo spit' – this is, in fact, a secretion produced by the froghopper bug and nothing whatever to do with cuckoos. Its scientific name *Cardamine* derives from the Greek *kardia*, meaning 'heart', and *damao subdue* refers to the plant's use in curing heart ailments. Culpepper declared Cuckoo Flower to be good for the treatment of scurvy and also for restoring a lost appetite. Its leaves, being very rich in vitamins and minerals, especially vitamin C, were frequently used in salads and also proved a useful addition to cough medicines. In Austria and France it was thought that anyone picking the flowers would soon after be bitten by an adder, whilst in Germany it was believed that bringing the plant indoors would cause the house to be struck by lightning

Pale Evening Dun
Procloeon bifidum (Plate 20)

This is a fairly widely distributed fly with a preference for the slower-flowing sections of rivers and streams. It is very similar to the Pale Watery and the same patterns can be used for both. The differences between them are that the Pale Evening Dun is slightly larger, a little paler in the abdomen and has no hindwings. The dun is mostly to be seen hatching towards dusk with the spinner actively egg-laying through the night. This makes the spinner of little use to the angler.

Nymph:
Size:	Up to 8mm
Colour:	Olive with pale markings
Type:	Agile darter

Adult:
Size:	Up to 7mm
Colour:	Dun: Female: pale yellow-olive abdomen, pale-grey wings, yellow-olive legs, olive-green eyes, grey-olive tails
Male: as female, but with yellow eyes
Spinner: Female: rich yellow abdomen, bright, clear wings with a tinge of green to the leading edge, pale-yellow legs, brown eyes, pale-yellow tails
Male: pale red-brown abdomen with last three segments orange-brown, bright, clear wings with a brownish tinge to leading edge, pale olive-brown legs, pale olive-brown eyes, grey tails
Habitat:	Chiefly the slower sections of streams and rivers
Distribution:	All over the British Isles, common in some areas, rare in others

Time of day:	Late evening or darkness
Time of year:	April–October, but main hatch July–August
Shape of rear wing:	None

Dressings

1. Pale Evening Dun (Kite)

DRESSING

Hook length: 8mm
Thread: White
Tail: Cream cock fibres
Abdomen: Grey goose fibres
Thorax: Grey goose doubled over
Hackle: Cream cock

2. Pale Evening Dun (Veniard)

DRESSING

Hook length: 8mm
Thread: Yellow
Tail: Honey dun fibres
Abdomen: Creamy seal's fur sub
Wing: Optional starling
Hackle: Honey dun

3. Pale Evening Dun Nymph (Sawyer)

DRESSING

Hook length: 9mm
Thread: None
Tail: Dyed olive goose
Abdomen: Yellow-brown dyed goose wound on with red wire
Thorax: As abdomen but wound with gold wire

Plate 20

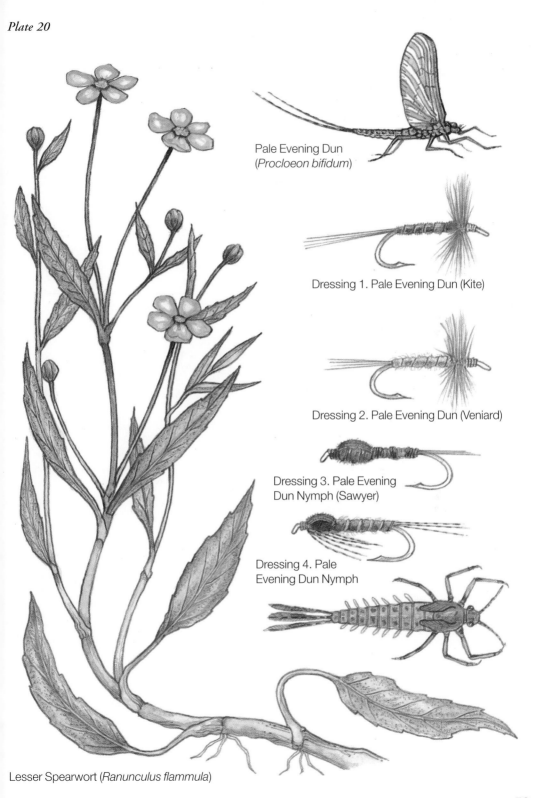

Pale Evening Dun
(*Procloeon bifidum*)

Dressing 1. Pale Evening Dun (Kite)

Dressing 2. Pale Evening Dun (Veniard)

Dressing 3. Pale Evening
Dun Nymph (Sawyer)

Dressing 4. Pale
Evening Dun Nymph

Lesser Spearwort (*Ranunculus flammula*)

4. Pale Evening Dun Nymph

DRESSING

Hook length: 9mm
Thread: Olive
Tail: Wood duck or partridge fibres
Abdomen: Pale olive-brown dubbing
Wingcase: Olive goose herls
Legs: Wood duck or partridge fibres

Lesser Spearwort
Ranunculus flammula (Plate 20)
Buttercup family (*Ranunculaceae*)

Flower head:	Typical small buttercup flowers, shiny yellow in appearance, up to 2cm wide and with 5 petals. They are carried singly or in loose clusters on long, furrowed stalks
Leaves:	Sparsely leafed; the narrow, undivided lance-shaped leaves are pointed and slightly toothed near the tip. Lower leaves are stalked, upper leaves unstalked
Flowering time:	May–September
Height:	Up to 70cm
Habit:	Native perennial
Habitat:	Wet places, streams, river banks, meadows, bogs
Distribution:	Common throughout
General:	This variable-looking plant can be either erect, spreading or prostrate in appearance, and the shape of the leaves may vary between sub-species. It is one of four British spearworts, all belonging to the buttercup family. *Ranunculus* derives from

the Latin *rana*, 'frog', a reference to these plants' liking for wet places. *Flammula* refers to spearwort's ability to cause inflammation of the skin. Like with all members of the buttercup family the sap of the plant contains poisons that cause blisters. Beggars used to apply the sap to their bodies to induce blistering and so evoke sympathy from passers-by. It has been know for livestock to die from eating Lesser Spearwort

Pale Watery
Baetis fuscatus (Plate 21)

In the past several species of fly were grouped under the name of Pale Watery because of their similarities: the Large and Small Spurwings, the Pale Evening Dun and the Small Dark Olive. The Pale Watery has a preference for weedy stretches of calcareous rivers where the duns hatch in open water and are readily taken by the trout. Hatches take place during the day and can be quite heavy. Swarming takes place mostly towards dusk and away from the water. The returning female spinner, known as the Golden Spinner, goes underwater to lay her eggs; the current then carries her body downstream, where she falls prey to waiting trout.

Nymph:	
Size:	Up to 9mm
Colour:	Sandy to dark olive
Type:	Agile darter
Adult:	
Size:	Up to 7mm
Colour:	Dun: Female: pale olive-grey

abdomen, pale-grey wings with pale-olive tinge, pale-olive legs, pale-green eyes, pale-grey tails
Male: similar but darker than the female and with yellow-orange eyes
Spinner: Female: golden-olive abdomen, bright, clear wings, pale-olive legs, red-brown eyes, pale-grey tails
Male: pale grey-white abdomen with last three segments orange-brown, red-brown thorax area, bright, clear wings, grey-white legs, pale-orange eyes, pale-grey tails

Habitat: Mostly weed stretches of calcareous rivers and streams
Distribution: Most parts of the British Isles
Time of day: Throughout the day
Time of year: May–September
Shape of rear wing: Very small oval with small coastal projection

Dressings

1. Pale Watery (Maryatt)

DRESSING

Hook length: 7mm
Thread: Yellow
Tail: Pale blue-dun fibres
Abdomen: Pale-yellow rabbit's fur or similar dubbing
Wings: Pale blue-dun hackle points
Hackle: Pale blue-dun cock

2. Last Hope (Goddard)

DRESSING

Hook length: 7mm
Thread: Pale yellow
Tail: Honey dun fibres
Abdomen: Buff-coloured herl (condor sub)
Wing: Optional starling
Hackle: Honey-dun cock

3. Pale Watery Nymph (Leisenring)

DRESSING

Hook length: 9mm
Thread: Primrose
Tail: Olive fibres
Abdomen: Opossum or Chinese mole fur
Rib: Gold wire
Thorax: As abdomen, built up
Legs: Dark blue-dun cock

4. Pale Watery Nymph (Sawyer)

DRESSING

Hook length: 9mm
Thread: None
Tail: Ginger cock fibres
Abdomen: Fawn darning wool and copper wire together
Thorax: As abdomen
Wingcase: Woodpigeon primary feather fibres
Legs: None

Plate 21

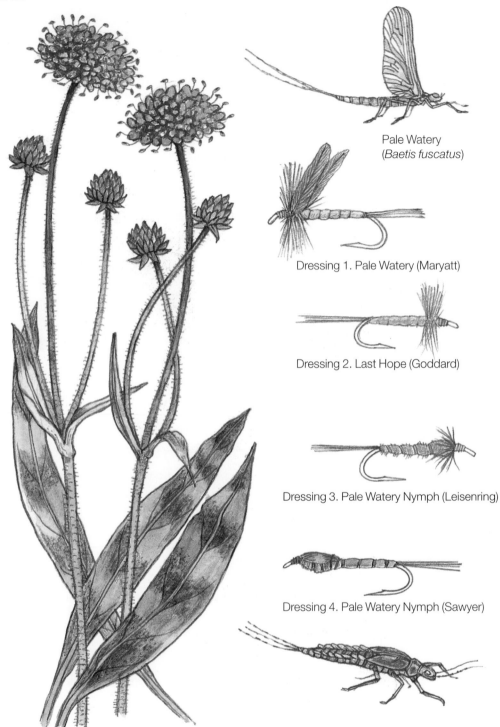

Pale Watery
(*Baetis fuscatus*)

Dressing 1. Pale Watery (Maryatt)

Dressing 2. Last Hope (Goddard)

Dressing 3. Pale Watery Nymph (Leisenring)

Dressing 4. Pale Watery Nymph (Sawyer)

Devil's Bit Scabious (*Succisa pratensis*)

62

Devil's Bit Scabious
Succisa pratensis (Plate 21)
Scabious family (*Dipsacaeae*)
(Blue Buttons)

Flower head:	Usually purplish-blue in colour although pale pinkish-white flowers may occur. Flowers are in dense hemispherical heads carried on stout, erect, bristly stems. Flowers in each head are the same size and between them are conspicuous protruding stamens
Leaves:	Dark green in colour and often blotched purple. Leaves are opposite, undivided and lance-shaped, the lower ones being on long stalks and having smooth margins, whereas the upper leaves are sometimes toothed
Flowering time:	June–October
Height:	Up to 100cm
Habit:	Perennial
Habitat:	Damp places, meadows and hedgerows
Distribution:	Common throughout
General:	This is the only bluish-purple scabious in the wild. It has a preference for either chalky or only slightly acid soils. The name 'scabious' refers to its former use in the treatment of scabies and other skin conditions. 'Devil's bit' is a reference to the story that the devil, in his anger at the plant's usefulness in curing ailments, bit off the end of the root in an attempt to get rid of it. Medicinally, the plant was used in the treatment of several conditions including plague, fever, poisoning and bruising. It is also a food source for a number of butterflies and moths and is occasionally used in ornamental gardens

Pond Olive
Cloeon dipterum (Plate 22)

This is a fairly widely distributed species and one of the more important flies to be found on the still waters. The Pond Olive can also be found on the slower stretches of rivers – I have found the odd spinner on a large, flat stretch of my local river. The imago is known as the Apricot Spinner and is unmistakable, the name denoting the rich apricot colour of the abdomen. The dun is not only variable in colour but also in size. The Pond Olive is unusual in that the eggs hatch inside the female spinner and, when released on the water surface, the nymph can swim away immediately.

Nymph:	
Size:	Up to 10mm
Colour:	Olive with brownish markings
Type:	Agile darter, preferring weed beds in shallower water
Adult:	
Size:	Up to 9mm
Colour:	Dun: Female: rich olive-brown abdomen, pale-grey wings, light-olive legs, green eyes, grey tails Male: olive-grey abdomen, pale-grey wings, grey-white legs, red-brown eyes, grey tails Spinner: Female: apricot abdomen, transparent ▶

Dressings

1. Pond Olive Dun (Price)

DRESSING

Hook length: 10mm
Thread: Olive
Tail: Blue-dun fibres
Abdomen: Olive goose herl
Rib: Brown thread
Wing: Blue-dun fibres tied upright
Hackle: Medium olive cock

2. Pond Olive Dun (Jardine)

DRESSING

Hook length: 10mm
Thread: Brown
Tail: Brown mallard fibres
Abdomen: Pale olive-brown herl
Rib: Gold wire
Wing: Cul-de-canard feather
Hackle: Honey-dun cock

3. Pond Olive Nymph (Walker)

DRESSING

Hook length: 10mm
Thread: Yellow
Tail: Brown partridge
Abdomen: Mix of ginger and brown seal's fur sub
Rib: Silver wire
Thorax: Brown seal's fur sub
Legs: Short-fibred honey hen hackle

4. Olive PVC (Goddard)

DRESSING

Hook length: 10mm
Thread: Yellow
Tail: Olive fibres (golden pheasant tip fibres dyed olive)
Abdomen: Olive fibres; the abdomen is then covered with clear PVC strip
Thorax: Olive-brown fibres
Wingcase: Pheasant tail fibres over thorax area

▶ wings with a pale-bronze leading edge, olive legs, pale olive-green eyes, brown tails Male: grey-cream abdomen with last three segments brown, transparent wings with brown leading edge, grey legs, red eyes, brown tails

Habitat: Still waters and very slow sections of rivers
Distribution: Fairly widespread
Time of day: Any time of day
Time of year: May–September
Shape of rear wing: None

Yellow Water-Lily
Nuphar lutea (Plate 22)
Water-Lily family (*Nymphaeaceae*) (Brandy Bottle)

Flower head: Solitary bowl-shaped flowers 10–20cm across held slightly above the water on stout stalks. Yellow in colour with a yellowy-green exterior made up of 4–6 thick sepals and numerous yellow stamens
Leaves: The thick, leathery leaves are almost circular in shape

Plate 22

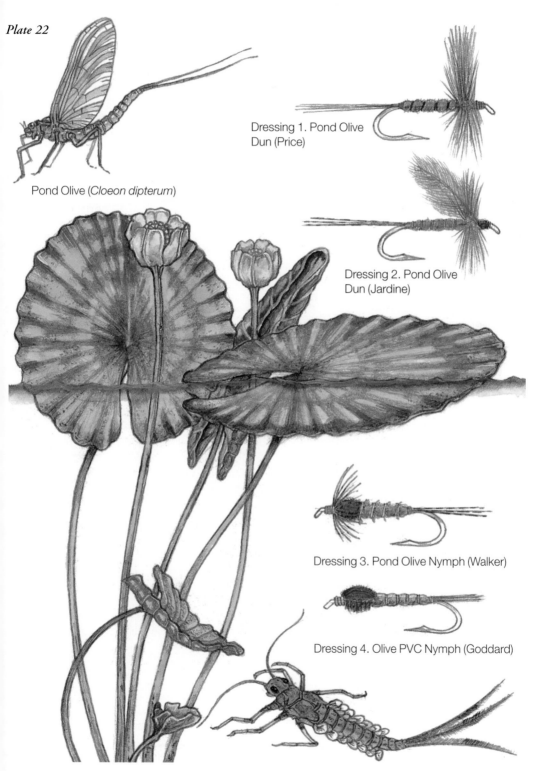

Pond Olive (*Cloeon dipterum*)

Dressing 1. Pond Olive
Dun (Price)

Dressing 2. Pond Olive
Dun (Jardine)

Dressing 3. Pond Olive Nymph (Walker)

Dressing 4. Olive PVC Nymph (Goddard)

Yellow Water-Lily (*Nuphar Lutea*)

with a heart-shaped basal notch. Deep green in colour and with a waxy outer surface, they float on the water at the end of rope-like stems often more than 2.5m long. The leaves themselves may be up to 30cm across and are the largest of any British water plant

Fruit: Flask-shaped capsule

Flowering time: June–August

Height: Up to 3m

Habit: Perennial

Habitat: Slow-flowing rivers, canals, ponds and lakes

Distribution: Fairly common throughout, but rarer in northern Scotland

General: A native perennial with a liking for cool water rich in nutrients. The scientific name *Nuphar* is derived from Arabic *naufar*, but the common name 'Brandy Bottle' is related to the flask-like shape of its seed capsule and also to the smell of stale alcohol given off by the flowers. During medieval times it was known as 'can-dock' – 'can' being a pottery vessel used for liquids. The seed capsule has air bladders in its tissues which allow the seed to remain afloat temporarily. Eventually the air is released and the seed sinks to the bottom to take root, so increasing the spread of the plant. Yellow Water-Lily was once thought to reduce sexual drive and described as a destroyer of pleasure and a poison of love. It was also seen as a symbol of purity, which probably explains its presence among carvings in many religious buildings, including Westminster Abbey and Lincoln Cathedral. According to German folklore the flowers were all water nymphs that changed from female form to flower whenever strangers passed by. Also beneath the leaves dwelt mischievous spirits waiting to take revenge on anyone picking the flowers. Medicinally the rhizome was said to be effective in curing the bite of a mad dog. Mixed with the rhizome of White Water-Lily and added to tar it was applied to the scalp to cure baldness. According to Culpepper, both leaves and flowers were used for curing inflammations, while a syrup made from the flowers could greatly assist in stilling a frantic mind

Purple Dun
Paraleptophlebia cincta
(Plate 23)

This is a rather uncommon fly found chiefly in reasonably fast-flowing rivers and streams with stony bottoms. In size and colour it is similar to, but a little larger than, the Iron Blue, the main difference being the shape of the rear wings. The Purple Dun has large, upright hindwings, the Iron Blue has small, oval ones. The Purple Dun has three tails and the Iron Blue two.

Nymph:
Size: Up to 10mm
Colour: Dull brown-green
Type: Laboured swimmer

Adult:
Size: Up to 8mm
Colour: Dun: Female: dull red-brown abdomen, dark-grey wings, olive-brown legs, dark-green eyes, grey tails
Male: dull grey-brown abdomen, dark-grey wings, red-brown wings, dark-brown eyes, grey tails
Spinner: Female: red-brown abdomen, transparent wings with brownish tinge, grey-brown legs, brown-black eyes, yellow tails
Male: grey-white abdomen with last three segments dark red-brown, similar-coloured thorax area, transparent wings with brown tinge, grey-brown legs, brown-black eyes, white tails
Habitat: Rivers and streams with a reasonable flow
Distribution: Uncommon and localized to areas in the west and north of England and Wales

Time of day: During daylight
Time of year: May–August
Shape of rear wing: Large, upright with coastal projection

Dressings

1. Purple Dun

DRESSING

Hook length: 8mm
Thread: Brown
Tail: Dun fibres
Abdomen: Red-brown dubbing
Wings: Dark-dun slips
Hackle: Dark-dun cock

2. Purple Dun (Veniard)

DRESSING

Hook length: 8mm
Thread: Purple
Tail: Dark-brown fibres
Abdomen: Purple wool
Wing: Starling
Hackle: Dark-brown hen

3. Purple Dun Nymph

DRESSING

Hook length: 10mm
Thread: Brown
Tail: Pheasant tail fibres
Abdomen: Dark-brown fur
Rib: Silver
Wingcase: Pheasant tail fibres over thorax and back

67

Plate 23

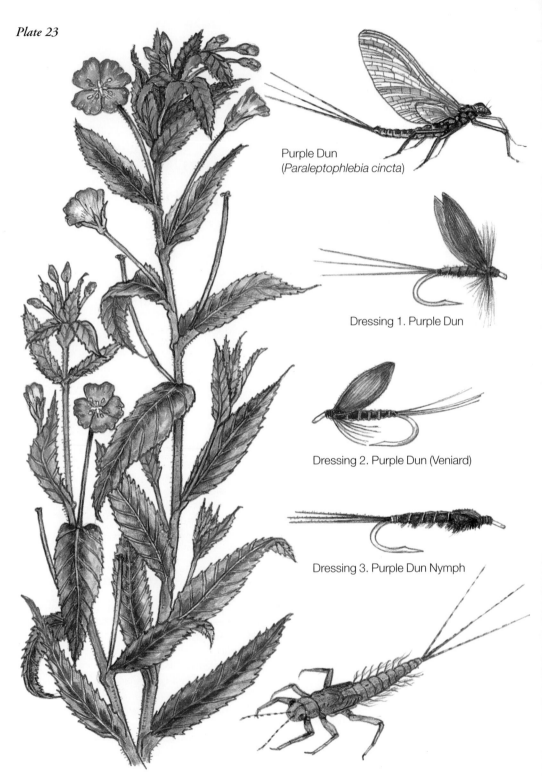

Purple Dun
(*Paraleptophlebia cincta*)

Dressing 1. Purple Dun

Dressing 2. Purple Dun (Veniard)

Dressing 3. Purple Dun Nymph

Great Willowherb (*Epilobium hirsutum*)

Great Willowherb
Epilobium hirsutum (Plate 23)
Willowherb family (*Onagraceae*)
(Codlins and Cream, Cherry Pie)

Flower head:	Single, large purplish-pink flowers, 2.5cm in diameter, held on stems coming from the junction of leaves and the main stems. Each flower is made up of 4 green sepals and 4 longer, slightly notched, overlapping petals. In the centre is a creamy 4-lobed stigma
Leaves:	Arranged in opposite pairs and half clasping the stem. Lower leaves are stalkless and have a slight downward curve. The spear-shaped leaves have a dense covering of fine hair and are slightly toothed
Flowering time:	June–September
Height:	Up to 2m
Habit:	Native perennial
Habitat:	Damp places, ditches, stream sides and marshes
Distribution:	Common throughout except western Scotland
General:	This is the tallest of the willowherbs. It is very similar to Hoary Willowherb, but is a much larger plant altogether. It is a very robust plant which spreads by means of fleshy roots just below the soil. It can and does form very extensive patches where it occurs to the exclusion of other plants. *Hirsutum* refers to the very hairy appearance of the plant. 'Codlins', which is an old word for a cooking apple, may be a

reference to the fragrance of the flowers and leaves when crushed, or 'codlins and cream' may refer to the rosy-coloured petals and cream central stigma

Sepia Dun
Leptophlebia marginata (Plate 24)

This is another dark-brown fly similar to the Claret Dun but is rarer, preferring still or slow-flowing water of a slightly acid nature. The nymph is reddish-brown and belongs in the group known as the laboured swimmers. The gills of the nymph are made up of a small plate and long filaments. When the nymph is ready to emerge as the dun it moves into the shallower water and crawls out onto waterside vegetation or stones. Another feature of the nymphs of the Claret and Sepia Duns are their exceptionally long and widespread tails. The main difference between the Sepia Dun and the Claret Dun in the adult stage is the wing colour – the Claret has very dark wings with contrasting paler rear wings, while the Sepia Dun's wings are both mid-brown in colour.

Nymph:	
Size:	Up to 12mm
Colour:	Reddish-brown
Type:	Laboured swimmer
Adult:	
Size:	Up to 10mm
Colour:	Dun: Female: dark, rich-brown abdomen, heavily veined brown wings giving olive-brown appearance, olive-brown legs, brown eyes, dark grey-brown tails Male: as female, but slightly darker Spinner: Female: rich red-

brown abdomen, clear wings with pale brown veins and grey areas to the front edge of the forewings, brown legs, dark-brown eyes, grey-brown tails Male: as female, but with slightly darker abdomen with distinct yellow-grey segmentation, and very dark olive eyes

Habitat: Still or slow-flowing acidic water
Distribution: Uncommon and localized throughout Britain
Time of day: Midday
Time of year: April–June
Shape of rear wing: Large, upright, no coastal projection

Dressings

1. Sepia Dun (Kite)

DRESSING
Hook length: 10mm
Thread: Dark brown
Tail: Brown cock fibres
Abdomen: Heron herls
Rib: Gold wire
Thorax: Heron herls doubled over
Hackle: Dark-brown cock

2. Sepia Nymph (Walker)

DRESSING
Hook length: 12mm
Thread: Black
Tail: Hen pheasant fibres
Abdomen: Brown-black wool picked out between rib
Rib: Black plastic strip
Thorax: Black floss
Wingcase: Dark pheasant tail fibres
Legs: Tips of wingcase tied under

3. Sepia Nymph (Jacques)

DRESSING
Hook length: 12mm
Thread: Maroon
Tail: Brown hackle fibres spaced apart
Abdomen: Cock pheasant fibres
Rib: Gold wire
Wingcase: Cock pheasant fibres
Legs: Honey or light-red fibres

Broad Leaved Pondweed
Potamogeton natans **(Plate 24)**
Pondweed family
(*Potamogetonaceae*)

Flower head: Individual flowers forming a stout, greenish-white spike up to 8cm long and held above water on a long stem. The inconspicuous flowers have no petals but are made up of 4 sepals around a stamen and style, and are about 4mm in diameter
Leaves: Two types of leaf occur – submerged and floating. Submerged leaves are very narrow and ribbonlike and under 3mm in width. The shiny, deep-green floating leaves are broad and leathery in appearance with numerous parallel veins. Oval in shape and with smooth margins that continue for a short way down the leaf stalk, they are held on long stems.
Flowering time: May–September
Height: Up to 1.5m
Habit: Perennial
Habitat: Shallow water less than 1m in depth, ponds, ditches

Plate 24

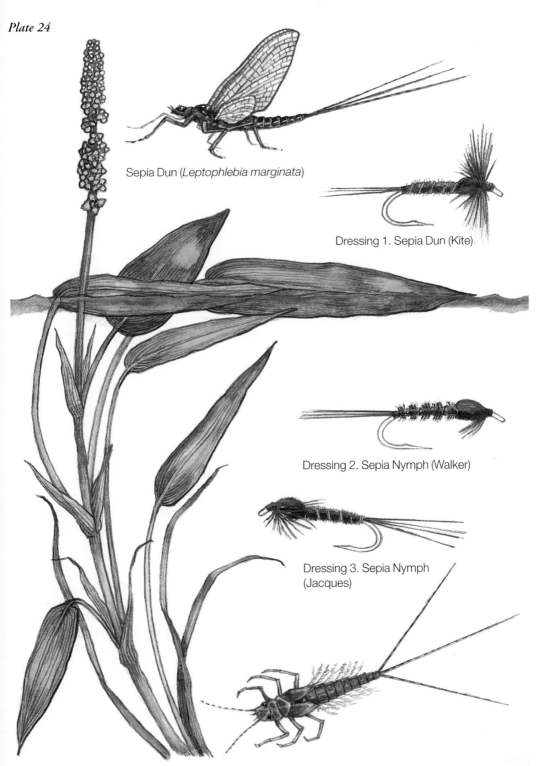

Sepia Dun (*Leptophlebia marginata*)

Dressing 1. Sepia Dun (Kite)

Dressing 2. Sepia Nymph (Walker)

Dressing 3. Sepia Nymph (Jacques)

Broad-Leaved Pondweed (*Potamogeton natans*)

and slow-moving rivers with rich organic mud

Distribution: Widespread

General: A vigorous, hairless aquatic which is one of a large family of pondweeds. Flowers are wind-pollinated and so have an inconspicuous appearance as there is no need to attract insects.

Potamogeton is derived from the Greek *potames* meaning 'river' and *geiton*, 'neighbour'. In East Anglia the plant is known as 'Fish Leaves' or 'Pickerel Weed' as it was thought that the floating leaves gave birth to young pike, or pickerel, which were often seen sheltering amongst them

Small Dark Olive
Baetis scambus (Plate 25)

This is a very small fly with a preference for streams and rivers with sand/gravel bottoms and good vegetation in alkaline water. It is a well distributed species throughout the British Isles and hatches can be prolific. The nymph is of the 'agile darter' group and emergence takes place in open water, mostly during the latter part of the day. Swarming takes place away from the water surface amongst trees, and in the spinner stage it is the returning female that is of most interest to the angler. On returning after mating, the female spinner goes underwater to lay her eggs. The dying body of the female then floats to the surface and is carried along with the current to the positioned trout.

Nymph:
Size: Up to 8mm

Colour: Sandy olive-green
Type: Agile darter

Adult:
Size: Up to 6mm
Colour: Dun: Female: pale-olive abdomen with last two segments yellowish-olive, pale-grey wings, pale-olive legs, black eyes, grey tails
Male: as female, but slightly darker and with dull red-brown eyes
Spinner: Female: rich-brown abdomen, clear wings with dark-grey veins, brown legs, black eyes, grey tails
Male: pale creamy-grey abdomen with last three segments orange-brown, bright, clear wings, pale-brown legs, red-brown eyes, grey tails

Habitat: Common throughout Britain on suitable rivers and streams
Distribution: Alkaline rivers and streams with good weed growth, preferably on sand/gravel
Time of day: Throughout the day
Time of year: The main hatch is from late May to August but they can be seen April–October
Shape of rear wing: Small, oval with small coastal projection

Dressings

1. July Dun (Veniard)

DRESSING

Hook length: 6mm
Thread: Pale yellow
Tail: Medium-olive fibres
Abdomen: Yellow heron herls
Rib: Gold wire
Hackle: Medium olive

Plate 25

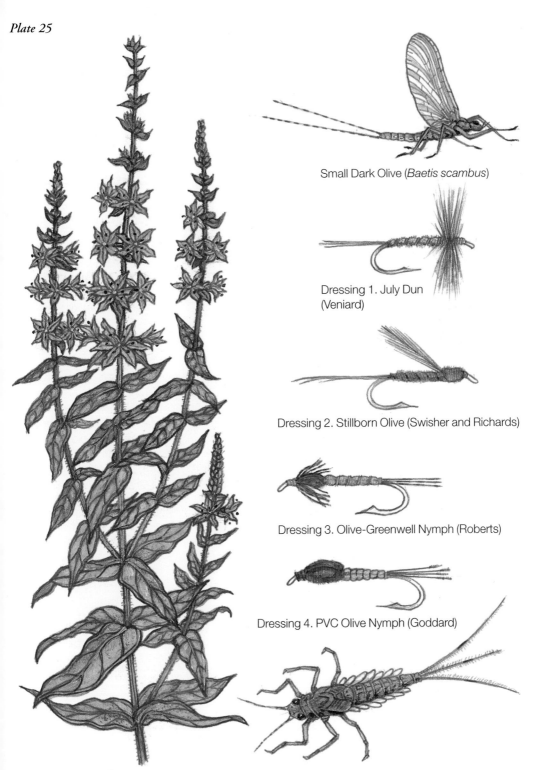

Small Dark Olive (*Baetis scambus*)

Dressing 1. July Dun
(Veniard)

Dressing 2. Stillborn Olive (Swisher and Richards)

Dressing 3. Olive-Greenwell Nymph (Roberts)

Dressing 4. PVC Olive Nymph (Goddard)

Purple Loosestrife (*Lythrum salicaria*)

2. Stillborn Olive (Swisher and Richards)

DRESSING

Hook length: 8mm
Thread: Olive
Tail/Shuck: A full medium-olive feather is used. The rear fibres are divided to make the tails and the rest of the fibres are pulled forwards and tied in at the hook bend
Abdomen: Pale-olive dubbing
Thorax: As abdomen but pronounced
Wings: Grey cock hackle tips

3. Olive-Greenwell Nymph (Roberts)

DRESSING

Hook length: 8mm
Thread: Yellow
Tail: Olive hackle fibres
Abdomen: Olive floss
Rib: Yellow thread
Thorax: Grey fur
Wingcase: Grouse hackle fibres over thorax
Legs: Ends of wingcase fibres turned under both sides

4. PVC Olive Nymph (Goddard)

DRESSING

Hook length: 8mm
Thread: Brown
Tail: Olive-green golden pheasant tips
Abdomen: Copper wire covered with olive-dyed heron herl then wound over with clear pvc strip
Thorax: Olive heron herl
Wingcase: Pheasant tail herl

Purple Loosestrife
Lythrum salicaria (Plate 25)
Loosestrife family (*Lythraceae*)
(Spiked Loosestrife)

Flower head:	Pinky-purple spike made up of 6 petalled star-shaped flowers carried in whorls of 6 around the stem. Petals have deeper vein colouring
Leaves:	Rich, green, lance-shaped leaves with short hairs at the edges and prominent veins. Leaves are stalkless, the upper ones growing in pairs at 90 degrees to each other, the lower in whorls of 3
Flowering time:	July–August
Height:	Up to 1.5m
Habit:	Native perennial
Habitat:	Marshes, reed swamps, beside lakes, slow rivers and canals
Distribution:	Common except in Scottish Highlands
General:	This tall, elegant plant is a familiar sight at the side of many waterways. Its name *salicaria* is a reference to the shape of its leaves, which are very willowlike – *Salix* being the Latin name of the willow family. Juices taken from the plant were sometimes used instead of oak bark for tanning leather as they are very rich in tannins. The leaves, which have antibacterial properties, were applied fresh to wounds to assist in healing

Small Spurwing
Centroptilum luteolum
(Plate 26)

The Small Spurwing was originally classed along with several other flies under the general heading of 'Pale Watery'. Although very similar to the Medium and Small Dark Olive and the now properly classified Pale Watery, *Baetis fuscatus*, identification can be made by examining the small hindwing, which has a small coastal projection in the shape of a spur. The fly has a preference for alkaline rivers, streams and lakes with sandy bottoms and good weed growth, and is often found in large numbers on chalk streams. The nymph is of the 'agile darter' group and hatches can occur throughout the day in open water. Because swarming takes place over and close to the water surface, male and female spinners become available to the trout. The female spinner lays her eggs by depositing them onto the water surface.

Nymph:
Size: Up to 9mm
Colour: Olive-grey-green
Type: Agile darter

Adult:
Size: Up to 7mm
Colour: Dun: Female: olive-grey abdomen, pale grey-blue wings, olive-grey legs, pale-green eyes, grey tails
Male: as female, but slightly darker and with orange-brown eyes
Spinner: Female: yellow-brown abdomen with pale segmentation, bright, transparent wings with a hint of pale olive, pale-olive legs, dark-olive eyes, grey-olive tails
Male: grey-white abdomen with last three segments pale orange-brown and orange-brown thorax area, wings as female, grey-olive legs, orange eyes, grey-white tails

Habitat: Mainly alkaline streams and rivers but also lakes with good weed growth
Distribution: Fairly common and widespread
Time of day: Throughout the day
Time of year: May–September but main hatches around June
Shape of rear wing: Small, oval with pointed coastal projection 'spur', and the tip is also pointed. In the Large Spurwing, *pennulatum*, the rear wing tip is rounded

Dressings

1. Light Cahill (Cahill)

DRESSING

Hook length: 7mm
Thread: Yellow
Tail: Cream cock fibres
Abdomen: Cream-olive seal's fur sub
Wing: Barred wood duck breast fibres
Hackle: Cream cock

2. Small Spurwing (Roberts)

DRESSING

Hook length: 7mm
Thread: Pale yellow
Tail: Cream cock fibres
Abdomen: Cream and pale-olive seal's fur mixed 3:1
Hackle: Pale blue-dun cock

Plate 26

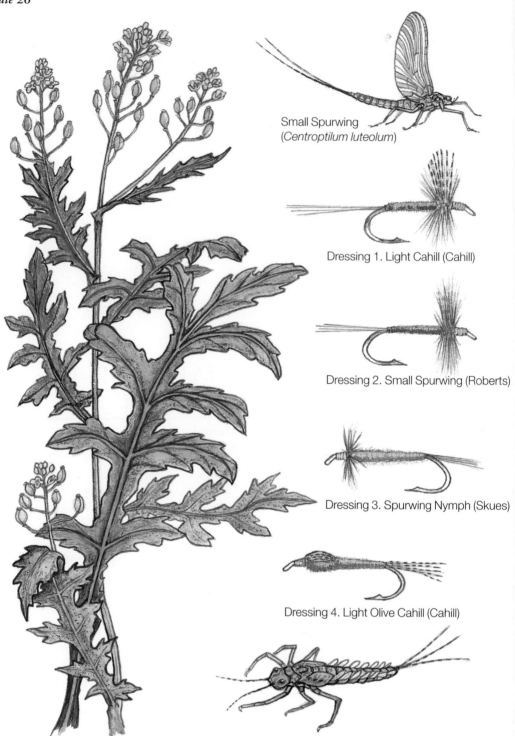

Small Spurwing
(*Centroptilum luteolum*)

Dressing 1. Light Cahill (Cahill)

Dressing 2. Small Spurwing (Roberts)

Dressing 3. Spurwing Nymph (Skues)

Dressing 4. Light Olive Cahill (Cahill)

Common Marsh Yellow Cress (*Rorippa palustris*)

3. Spurwing Nymph (Skues)

DRESSING

Hook length: 9mm
Thread: White
Tail: Pale-blue hen fibres
Abdomen: Pale-olive wool
Hackle: Dark-blue short-fibred cock

4. Light Olive Cahill Nymph (Cahill)

DRESSING

Hook length: 9mm
Thread: Pale grey
Tail: Mandarin duck fibres
Abdomen: Pale olive-grey wool
Wingcase: Mandarin duck fibres over thorax area

Marsh Yellow Cress
Rorippa palustris (Plate 26)
Cress family (*Cruciferae*)

Flower head:	Yellow flowers carried at the end of erect hollow stems and made up of 4 petals and sepals of equal length
Leaves:	Deeply lobed, hairless leaves; the lower ones are stalked but upper ones may be stalkless. The base of each leaf stalk half clasps the stem
Flowering time:	June–September
Height:	Up to 60cm
Habit:	Annual or biennial
Habitat:	Pond sides, river banks and water meadows, but occasionally drier areas
Distribution:	Common

General: Marsh Yellow Cress is a member of the cabbage family and one of four types of yellow cress to be found in Britain. It is also related to watercress but, unlike that plant, it is inedible. Like all members of the cabbage family the four petals are in the shape of a cross. Although the name *palustris* means 'growing in marshes', yellow cress prefers areas that are wet in winter yet dry out to some extent in summer and, as such can be a pest of cultivated areas

Turkey Brown
Paraleptophlebia submarginata (Plate 27)

This is a medium-sized fly with a very dark overall appearance: the abdomen is dark brown-black and the wings are heavily veined with shaded areas to the cross veins. A small area in the centre of the wing is devoid of these cross veins, leaving a distinct pale area. This species is reasonably well distributed but hatches are localized and sparse. It is one of the upwinged flies that is of little interest from a fishing point of view and so no specific imitations have been devised. Nymphs of the Turkey Brown fall into the group known as the 'laboured swimmers' and are reddish-grey-brown and chiefly found in stony rivers and streams. When ready to emerge, the nymph crawls out of the water onto vegetation or a stone.

Nymph:	
Size:	Up to 12mm
Colour:	Reddish-grey-brown
Type:	Laboured swimmer

Adult:
Size: Up to 10mm
Colour: Dun: Female: dark-brown abdomen, olive-brown wings with dark brown veins and shaded areas to the cross veins but with distinctly pale vein-free central area, olive-brown legs, brown-black eyes, dark-brown tails
Male: overall even darker than the female; the wings are similar and the eyes are dull red-brown
Spinner: Female: dark red-brown abdomen with pale segmentation, bright wings with pale olive-brown veins, olive-brown legs, pale-brown eyes, grey-brown tails
Male: grey-brown abdomen with last three segments red-brown and pale-grey segmentation, bright, transparent wings with pale olive-brown veins, dark-brown legs, dark red-brown eyes, pale grey-brown tails
Habitat: Mostly found on reasonably fast stony rivers and streams
Distribution: Throughout Britain but localized and very sparse
Time of day: Midday onwards
Time of year: May–July but in any one particular location over just a few weeks at most and not at all prolific
Shape of rear wing: Large, upright, no coastal projection

Dressings

1. Turkey Brown Dun

DRESSING

Hook length: 10mm
Thread: Dark brown
Tail: Dark-brown cock fibres
Abdomen: Dark brown seal's fur and hare's ear fur dubbed together
Rib: Gold wire
Wing: Hen pheasant
Hackle: Dark-brown cock

2. Turkey Brown Nymph

DRESSING

Hook length: 12mm
Thread: Dark brown
Tail: Cock pheasant tail fibres
Abdomen: Heron herl
Rib: Silver wire
Wingcase and top of abdomen: Cock pheasant tail fibres
Legs: Pheasant tail fibres

3. *Paraleptophlebia* Nymph

DRESSING

Hook length: 12mm
Thread: Black
Tail: Brown mallard
Abdomen: Red-brown seal's fur sub
Rib: Silver wire
Thorax: Brown-black seal's fur sub
Wingcase: Brown mallard
Legs: Brown partridge

Plate 27

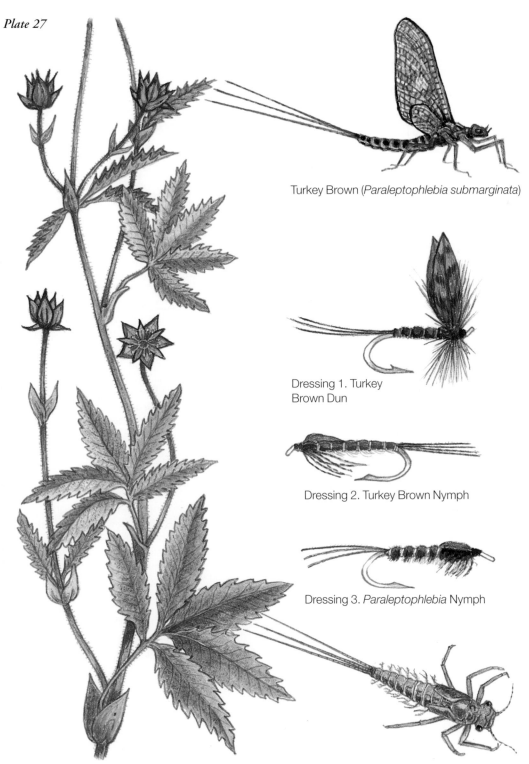

Turkey Brown (*Paraleptophlebia submarginata*)

Dressing 1. Turkey Brown Dun

Dressing 2. Turkey Brown Nymph

Dressing 3. *Paraleptophlebia* Nymph

Marsh Cinquefoil (*Potentilla palustris*)

Marsh Cinquefoil
Potentilla palustris (**Plate 27**)
Rose family (*Rosaceae*)
(Bog Strawberry)

Flower head:	Branched clusters of small purple, almost brownish-red florets. Each is made up of 5 petals and 5 sepals, the petals being smaller and slightly hairy
Leaves:	Long-stalked leaves, greyish-green in colour, made up of 5–7 leaflets serrated at the edges
Flowering time:	May–July
Height:	Up to 45cm
Habit:	Native perennial
Habitat:	Fens, marshes, bogs and wet ground
Distribution:	Fairly common throughout but more so in the north
General:	This is the only purple-coloured cinquefoil to be found in Britain – the others are the more usual yellow colour. Cinquefoil is a French name meaning 'five leaves' and is derived from the groups of five leaflets. As its name suggests, it is a plant of boggy wet ground. *Potentilla* comes from the Latin *potens*, meaning 'powerful', and refers to the plant's many medicinal properties

Yellow Evening Dun
Ephemerella notata (**Plate 28**)

This fly is very similar to *Heptagenia sulphurea*, the Yellow May Dun, but it is slightly smaller and has three tails, not two. It is also a lot less common than the Yellow May Dun and has a short hatch period, from May to June. The nymph is of the 'moss creeper' group and only four pairs of plate-like gills are visible. Emergence takes place in open water from midday onwards. The returning female spinner deposits her eggs onto the water and after egg-laying falls spent on the surface. From a fishing point of view this fly is of limited interest only in the localized areas where it is found.

Nymph:	
Size:	Up to 10mm
Colour:	Yellow-olive-brown, often with contrasting markings
Type:	Moss-crawler
Adult:	
Size:	Up to 10mm
Colour:	Dun: Female: yellow abdomen, pale yellow-grey wings, yellow legs, green eyes, yellow tails
	Male: yellow abdomen with last three segments orange-brown, pale yellow-grey wings, yellow legs, orange eyes, yellow tails
	Spinner: Female: yellow abdomen, bright, transparent wings with yellow tinge to leading edges, yellow legs, green eyes, olive tails
	Male: as female, but with orange-yellow eyes
Habitat:	Moderately fast-flowing rivers
Distribution:	In the West, particularly Wales, and in parts of Ireland but not Scotland
Time of day:	Midday onwards

Plate 28

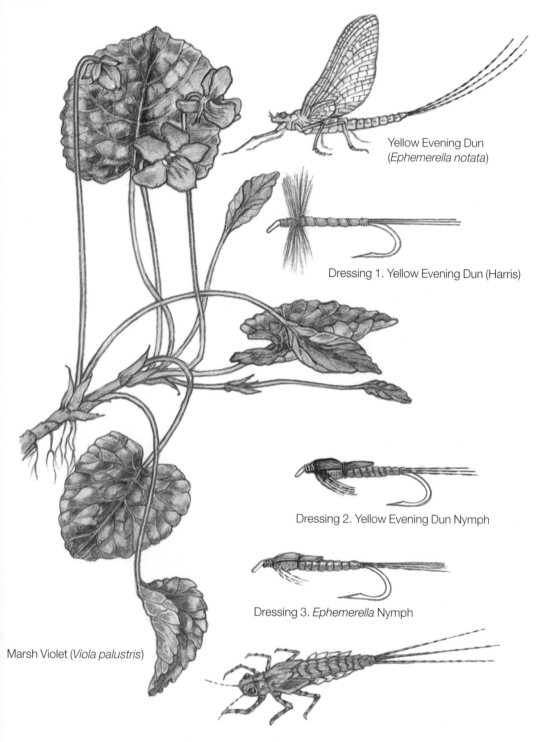

Yellow Evening Dun
(*Ephemerella notata*)

Dressing 1. Yellow Evening Dun (Harris)

Dressing 2. Yellow Evening Dun Nymph

Dressing 3. *Ephemerella* Nymph

Marsh Violet (*Viola palustris*)

Time of year: May–June
Shape of rear wing: Large, upright with coastal projection

Dressings

1. Yellow Evening Dun (Harris)

DRESSING

Hook length: 10mm
Thread: Orange
Tails: Ginger cock fibres
Abdomen: Orange-yellow floss
Rib: Gold wire
Wing: Cock fibres dyed yellow
Hackle: Ginger cock

2. Yellow Evening Dun Nymph

DRESSING

Hook length: 10mm
Thread: Olive-yellow
Tail: Olive-yellow cock fibres
Abdomen: Olive-brown seal's fur sub
Rib: Thread
Wingcase/gill cover: Brown feather fibres
Legs: Brown partridge fibres

3. *Ephemerella* Nymph

DRESSING

Hook length: 10mm
Thread: Brown
Tail: Olive-brown cock fibres
Abdomen: Olive-brown seal's fur sub covered with clear pvc strip
Thorax: As abdomen
Wingcase/gill cover: Brown partridge or pheasant tail fibres
Legs: Brown partridge fibres

Marsh Violet
Viola palustris (Plate 28)
Violet family (*Violaceae*)
(Bog Violet)

Flower head: Single lilac flowers with darker purple veining and a short pale-lilac spur, 10–15mm across
Leaves: Long-stalked, broad, kidney-shaped leaves, shallowly lobed and hairless
Flowering time: April–July
Height: Up to 8cm
Habit: Perennial
Habitat: Marshes, wet heaths and boggy ground
Distribution: Throughout, but commoner in the north and west
General: This easily identified member of the violet family is always found growing in wet soils that are low in nutrients. Some medicinal properties it has are in the relief of chest congestion and rheumatic pains

Yellow May Dun
Heptagenia sulphurea
(Plate 29)

Distribution:	Fairly widespread
Time of day:	Midday to dusk
Time of year:	May–July
Shape of rear wing:	Large upright with coastal projections

It is said that the Yellow May Dun is not popular with fish and if alternatives are available they will be taken in preference. The truth may simply be, however, that the hatches are so sparse the fish never get the chance to take the fly in obvious numbers. The colour may be another factor. The only other fly with a comparable appearance is the Yellow Evening Dun, but this is smaller and with three tails, not two. Although the Yellow May Dun is found on chalk streams it is more common on faster-flowing rivers. The egg-laying spinners are likely to be of more interest to the fish than the dun when, after mating, they return to the water in more reasonable numbers to lay their eggs.

Nymph:
Size:	Up to 15mm
Colour:	Olive-brown
Type:	Stone/weed-clinger

Adult:
Size:	Up to 12mm
Colour:	Dun: Female: pale-yellow abdomen, pale-yellow wings with very pale-brown veins, pale-yellow legs, pale-blue eyes, grey tails
	Male: pale-yellow abdomen, pale-yellow wings with pale-brown veins, pale-yellow legs, pale-blue eyes, grey tails
	Spinner: Female: golden-yellow abdomen, transparent wings with very pale yellow leading edge, light-olive legs, pale-blue eyes, grey tails
	Male: rich yellow-brown abdomen, transparent wings veined grey-brown, yellow-brown legs, blue eyes, grey-brown tails
Habitat:	Rivers

Dressings
1. Yellow May Dun (Weaver)

> **DRESSING**
>
> **Hook length**: 12mm
> **Thread**: Yellow
> **Tail**: Golden-yellow antron wool
> **Abdomen**: SLF colour MC7
> **Wing**: Pale natural deer hair

2. Yellow May Nymph

> **DRESSING**
>
> **Hook length**: 14mm
> **Thread**: Orange-brown
> **Tail**: Brown mallard
> **Abdomen**: Pale yellow-brown fur
> **Rib**: Gold wire
> **Thorax**: Brown fur
> **Wingcase**: Pheasant tail fibres
> **Legs**: Wingcase tips turned under

3. Yellow May Dun Nymph (Edwards)

> **DRESSING**
>
> **Hook length**: 14mm
> **Thread**: Yellow
> **Tail**: Grey partridge dyed pale yellow
> **Abdomen**: Fur dyed pale yellow and then covered with polythene strip
> **Thorax**: Fur dyed pale yellow
> **Wingcase**: Grey partridge dyed yellow
> **Wing buds**: Pale-brown raffene cut to shape
> **Legs**: Grey partridge dyed yellow

Plate 29

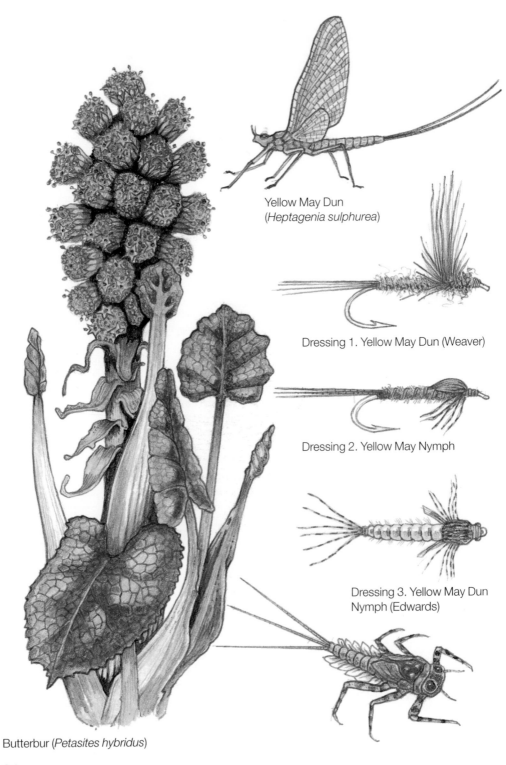

Yellow May Dun
(*Heptagenia sulphurea*)

Dressing 1. Yellow May Dun (Weaver)

Dressing 2. Yellow May Nymph

Dressing 3. Yellow May Dun
Nymph (Edwards)

Butterbur (*Petasites hybridus*)

Butterbur
Petasites hybridus (Plate 29)
Daisy family (*Compositae*)
(Sweet Coltsfoot, Bog Rhubarb)

Flower head: A dense erect spike up to 40cm high appearing in early spring before the leaves. The stem, which is hollow and purplish in colour, has a rather scaly appearance. The unscented flower head is made up of many 5-toothed flowers, pink to blush red in colour depending on the soil in which the plant is growing. Male and female flowers are on separate plants, the male being far more common than the female

Leaves: Appearing shortly after the flowers and growing to a great size – as much as 90cm across. The leaves are rounded with a heart-shaped base, toothed margins and grow on long, hollow leaf stalks. The undersides of the leaves are covered with a dense grey felting of hairs

Fruit: Single-seeded with a parachute of hairs similar to those of a dandelion clock

Flowering time: March–April

Height: Up to 150cm

Habit: Perennial

Habitat: Riverbanks, watersides, muddy soils and wet places

Distribution: The male plant is common throughout Britain but the female is very limited in its distribution

General: Butterbur is a patch-forming perennial which spreads by means of thick, creeping rhizomes growing up to 1.5m in length. Its most noticeable feature is its huge leaves, of which sixteenth-century herbalist John Gerard said they were big enough to keep a man's head from rain and from the heat of the sun. Its name *Petasites* is taken from the Greek *petasos*, meaning a 'broad-brimmed hat'. In France it is referred to as *chapeau du diable* – the devil's hat. English tradition has it that the huge leaves were used for wrapping butter, hence its common name 'Butterbur'. The leaves actually have antispasmodic properties and are used in herbalism. Culpepper, the seventeenth-century herbalist, recommended that its root be used as a cure for fevers, plague and all spots and blemishes. Taken in wine, he said, the root would resist the power of any other poison. In more modern times extracts from Butterbur are used for curing headaches and neuralgia, and also as a heart tonic

The Upwinged Fly Nymphs

The Burrowers
Ephemera (Plate 30)
Mayfly

This is the largest of the upwinged nymphs, being up to 25mm long. These nymphs burrow into fine gravel, mud or sand on the river bed. The mandibles and gills are particularly designed for creating and living in the tunnels which they form. The colour of the nymph is cream with contrasting darker markings. Three species occur in Britain: *danica*, *vulgata* and *lineata*. *Danica* prefers faster-flowing rivers and streams, also lakes with fine gravel or sandy beds. *Vulgata* prefers slower rivers and small still waters with muddy bottoms. *Lineata* is rare and is confined to a few of the larger rivers. The same patterns will do for all species. It must be remembered that, because of its lifestyle, the nymph is only active above ground – and available to the trout – for a short time before the actual Mayfly hatch. Having said this, many patterns do exist to represent the nymph.

Dressings
1. Mayfly Nymph (Masters)

DRESSING

Hook length: Up to 20mm
Thread: Brown
Tail: Pheasant tail fibres
Abdomen: Cream llama wool
Rib: Thread
Wingcase: Pheasant tail fibres
Legs: Brown nylon cut to length

2. Emerger Mayfly (Jardine)

DRESSING

Hook length: Up to 20mm
Thread: Brown
Tail: Cock pheasant fibres
Abdomen: Cream furry foam
Rib: Brown thread
Thorax: Brown rabbit's fur and pearlescent spedraflash
Wing: Deer hair

3. Mayfly Nymph (Walkers)

DRESSING

Hook length: Up to 20mm
Thread: Brown
Tail: Pheasant tail fibres
Abdomen: Light-buff angora wool
Rib: Pheasant tail fibres
Thorax: As abdomen but picked out
Wingcase: Pheasant tail fibres
Legs: Wingcase fibres turned under

4. Stillborn Mayfly (Orvis)

DRESSING

Hook length: Up to 20mm
Thread: Brown
Tail: Hare fibres
Abdomen: Cream antron
Rib: Brown floss
Thorax: Cream antron
Wingcase: Deer hair
Legs: Tips of deer hair left both sides of thorax

Plate 30

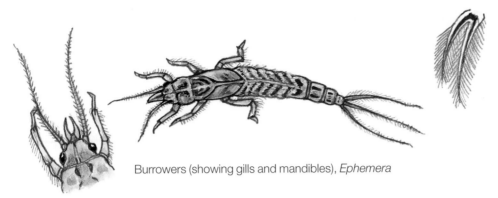

Burrowers (showing gills and mandibles), *Ephemera*

Dressing 1. Mayfly Nymph (Masters)

Dressing 2. Emerger Mayfly (Jardine)

Dressing 3. Mayfly Nymph (Walker)

Dressing 4. Stillborn Mayfly (Orvis)

Dressing 5. Swimming Mayfly Nymph (Price)

Dressing 6. Suspender Mayfly Nymph
(Goddard and Clarke)

Dressing 7. Mayfly Emerger (Price)

Dressing 8. Mayfly Nymph (Veniard)

5. Swimming Mayfly Nymph (Price)

DRESSING

Hook length: Up to 20mm
Thread: Brown
Tail: Cock pheasant tail fibres
Abdomen: Cream wool
Rib: Brown thread
Thorax: Cream wool
Gills: Tuft of brown marabou tied in rear of wingcase
Wingcase: Cock pheasant fibres
Legs: Wingcase fibres turned under

6. Suspender Mayfly Nymph (Goddard and Clarke)

DRESSING

Hook length: Up to 20mm
Thread: Brown
Tail: Three cream ostrich herl tips
Abdomen: White, tan, yellow seal's fur sub (2:1:1)
Rib: Brown thread
Thorax: Brown thread
Wingcase: A small ethafoam ball in nylon mesh coloured brown

7. Mayfly Emerger (Price)

DRESSING

Hook length: Up to 20mm
Thread: Brown
Tail: Cock pheasant tail
Abdomen: Cream dubbing
Rib: Brown thread
Thorax: Cream-olive dubbing
Emerging wing: Cul-de-canard feathers tied in a head and rear of thorax

8. Mayfly Nymph (Veniard)

DRESSING

Hook length: Up to 20mm
Thread: Brown
Tail: Cock pheasant fibres
Abdomen: Back half yellow-grey seal's fur sub; front half pale olive-brown seal's fur sub
Rib: Brown thread
Thorax: Pale olive-brown seal's fur sub
Wingcase: Dark-brown partridge fibres
Legs: Ends of wingcase tied under

The Silt-Dwellers
Caenis and *Brachycercus* (Plate 31)

These are the smallest of the upwinged flies and number six *caenis* species and one *brachycercus*, but they are so very similar for fishing purposes that they are treated as one. Because of the prolific hatches and their tiny size they are often referred to as the 'angler's curse'. The fact that the nymphs are so small live in the silt or mud on the bottom makes it almost impossible to fish the artificial in a natural manner. Many patterns do exist but they vary widely in colour, which may be due because the natural becomes covered with silt particles from the bottom on which it lives. The natural colour is an olive to rich brown, at times with contrasting markings. Only the first pair of gills are visible and these are very small, the rest being covered with the second pair of gills which are so enlarged that they form gill covers.

Plate 31

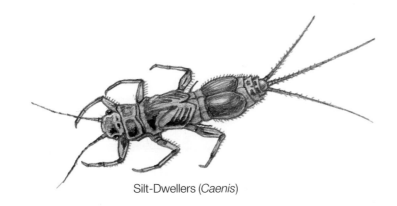

Silt-Dwellers (*Caenis*)

Dressing 1. Pale Emerger (Price)

Dressing 2. Pheasant Tail (Sawyer)

Dressing 3. *Caenis* Nymph

Dressing 4. *Caenis* Nymph (Carnill)

Dressing 5. *Caenis* Nymph (US)

Dressing 6. Trico Nymph (US)

Dressing 7. Grey Goose Nymph (Sawyer)

Dressing 8. *Caenis* Nymph (Roberts)

Dressings

1. Pale Emerger (Price)

DRESSING

Hook length: 6mm
Thread: Pale yellow
Tail: Brown feather fibres
Abdomen: Very pale yellow dubbing
Rib: Fine gold wire
Thorax: As abdomen
Emerging wing: Small cul-de-canard feathers over thorax area

2. Pheasant Tail (Sawyer)

DRESSING

Hook length: 6mm
Tail: Cock pheasant fibres
Abdomen: Cock pheasant fibres
Rib: Fine copper wire
Wingcase: Pheasant tail fibres doubled over thorax area

3. *Caenis* Nymph

DRESSING

Hook length: 6mm
Thread: Brown
Tail: Partridge fibres
Abdomen: Cream fur
Rib: Fine brown thread
Thorax: As abdomen
Wingcase: Partridge fibres
Legs: Partridge fibres

4. *Caenis* Nymph (Carnill)

DRESSING

Hook length: 6mm
Thread: Brown
Tail: Brown partridge fibres
Abdomen: Dull brown-grey herl, heron or similar
Rib: Stripped peacock quill
Thorax: Hare's ear fur
Wingcase/gill cover: Biot quill from heron primary feather cut to shape over half the abdomen
Legs: Partridge fibres

5. *Caenis* Nymph (America)

DRESSING

Hook length: 6mm
Thread: Brown
Tail: Cock pheasant fibres
Abdomen: Grey-brown dubbing
Rib: Fine brown thread
Wingcase: Black rabbit fur
Legs: Thorax area picked out

6. Trico Nymph (America)

DRESSING

Hook length: 6mm
Thread: Brown
Tail: Cock pheasant fibres
Abdomen: Pale brown dubbing
Legs: Dubbing picked out in thorax area

7. Grey Goose Nymph (Sawyer)

DRESSING

Hook length: 6mm
Thread: None
Tail: Grey goose fibres
Abdomen: Grey goose fibres
Rib: Fine copper wire
Thorax: As abdomen
Wingcase: Grey goose fibres doubled over thorax area

8. *Caenis* Nymph (Roberts)

DRESSING

Hook length: 6mm
Thread: White
Tail: Brown partridge
Abdomen: Cream seal's fur sub
Rib: Fine silver wire
Legs: Grey partridge

The Moss- and Weed-Crawlers

Ephemerella (Plate 32)

Blue-Winged Olive, Yellow Evening Dun

The *Ephemerella* nymphs have a slightly flattened appearance and the gills are in the shape of small plates with only four pairs visible. They grow to about 10mm in length and are usually gingery-brown-olive in appearance with contrasting markings, especially to the legs. They spend most of their time crawling around amongst the moss, stones and vegetation on the river bed. Of the two species that make up the group, the Blue-Winged Olive is by far the most abundant and is active over a much longer period than *Ephemerella notata*, the Yellow Evening Dun. The latter is a very uncommon and localized species. The Blue-Winged Olive is found in varied habitats from rivers to still waters. The Yellow Evening Dun is a fly of moderately fast-flowing rivers.

Dressings

1. Natant Nymph (Brookes)

DRESSING

Hook length: 10mm
Thread: Brown
Tail: Grouse hackle fibres
Abdomen: Tan wool
Rib: Gold wire
Thorax: As abdomen
Wingcase: Ball of ethafoam encased in nylon mesh, grey or tan coloured
Legs: Grouse hackle fibres

2. Floating Nymph (Jardine)

DRESSING

Hook length: 10mm
Thread: Brown
Tail: Wood duck fibres
Abdomen: Dark-olive antron
Rib: Thin fibres from white string
Thorax: As abdomen
Wing: Poly wing, grey coloured
Legs: Olive cock parachute

Plate 32

Moss- and Weed-Crawlers (*Ephemerella*)

Dressing 1. Natant Nymph (Brookes)

Dressing 2. Floating Nymph (Jardine)

Dressing 3. Blue-Winged Olive Nymph (Jacobsen)

Dressing 4. Blue-Winged Olive Nymph (US)

Dressing 5. Blue-Winged Olive Nymph (Price)

Dressing 6. Blue-Winged Olive Nymph (Edwards)

Dressing 7. Hendrickson Nymph (Steenrod)

Dressing 8. Blue-Winged Olive Nymph (UK)

3. Blue-Winged Olive Nymph (Jacobsen)

DRESSING

Hook length: 10mm
Thread: Orange
Tail: Brown-speckled partridge fibres
Abdomen: Rust antron and hare mixed
Thorax: Black cow's hair
Legs: Short dark blue-dun hackle

4. Blue-Winged Olive Nymph (US)

DRESSING

Hook length: 10mm
Thread: Brown
Tail: Brown mallard fibres dyed olive
Abdomen: Olive-dyed rabbit's fur
Rib: Brown thread
Thorax: As abdomen
Legs: Brown mallard fibres dyed olive

5. Blue-Winged Olive Nymph (Price)

DRESSING

Hook length: 10mm
Thread: Olive
Tail: Olive-dyed grizzle cock fibres
Abdomen: Antron or fur dyed medium olive
Rib: Transparent olive swannundaze
Thorax: As body
Wingcase/wingbuds: Recording tape tied over thorax and cut to shape to form two wingbuds extending over half the abdomen
Legs: Partridge dyed olive

6. Blue-Winged Olive Nymph (Edwards)

DRESSING

Hook length: 10mm
Thread: Orange
Tail: Dark partridge well marked
Abdomen: Sandy hare's ear
Rib: Gold wire
Thorax: As abdomen
Wingcase: Pheasant tail fibres in two bunches either side of thorax area
Legs: Dark partridge well marked

7. Hendrickson (Steenrod)

DRESSING

Hook length: 10mm
Thread: Olive-brown
Tail: Wood duck flank fibres
Abdomen: Grey-brown fur
Rib: Brown floss
Thorax: As abdomen
Wingcase: Dark-brown well-marked feather fibres
Legs: Wingcase fibres turned under

8. Blue-Winged Olive Nymph (UK)

DRESSING

Hook length: 10mm
Thread: Olive
Tail: Olive grizzle fibres
Abdomen: Olive heron herls
Rib: Gold wire
Thorax: Olive seal's fur
Wingcase: Olive feather fibres
Legs: Olive grizzle hackle

The Stone-Clingers

Ecdyonorus, Rhithrogena, Heptagenia (Plate 33)

Amongst this group are four *Ecdyonorus* species: *Ecdyonorus dispar*, the Autumn Dun, *Ecdyonorus torrentis*, the Large Brook Dun, *Ecdyonorus insignis*, the Large Green Dun and *Ecdyonorus venosus*, the Late March Brown; two from the *Rhithrogena*: *Rhithrogena germanica*, the March Brown and *Rhithrogena semicolorata*, the Olive Upright; four from the *Heptagenia*: *Heptagenia lateralis*, the Dusky Yellowstreak, *Heptagenia sulphurea*, the Yellow May Dun, and two others, *longicauda* and *fuscogrisea*, not dealt with in this book because of their extreme rarity.

Although the list is fairly long the nymphs are basically of a similar shape and habit. They are called stone-clingers because that is just what they do. The nymphs have broad, flattened bodies capable of living amongst stones and boulders even in the strongest of currents. The body is designed so that water pressure helps to keep the nymph pressed downwards. The nymphs can, with the help of their strong limbs, move rapidly across the surface of the stones, always keeping their head and shoulders facing upstream.

Although chiefly a nymph of stony streams and rivers, some species are also found on the stony shores of lakes. Colours vary from dull olive-greens to dark browns with contrasting markings.

Dressings

1. March Brown Floating Nymph (Jardine)

DRESSING

Hook length: Up to 15mm
Thread: Brown
Tail: Lemon wood duck
Abdomen: Dubbed hare's fur
Emerging wing: Antron floss

2. Emerging Nymph (Jardine)

DRESSING

Hook length: 15mm
Thread: Brown
Tail: Deer hair fibres
Abdomen: Deer hair dubbed
Rib: Gold wire
Emerging wing: Antron floss

3. Ecdyonorus Nymph (Edwards)

DRESSING

Hook length: Up to 15mm
Thread: Olive
Tail: Moose mane hairs spread
Abdomen: Yellow-olive-brown fur
Rib: Gold wire
Thorax: As abdomen
Wingcase: Cock pheasant fibres over thorax
Legs: Speckled partridge cut to length
Head cover: Brown raffene

4. Gold Ribbed Hare's Ear

DRESSING

Hook length: Up to 15mm
Thread: Brown
Tail: Hare's ear guard hairs
Abdomen: Hare's ear mixed shades, preferably dark
Rib: Gold wire
Thorax: As abdomen
Legs: Long thorax hairs picked out

Plate 33

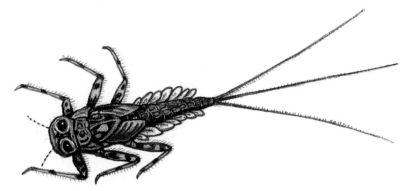

Stone-Clingers (*Ecdyonorus*, *Rhithrogena*, *Heptagenia*)

Dressing 1. March Brown Floating Nymph
(Jardine)

Dressing 2. Emerging Nymph (Jardine)

Dressing 3. *Ecdyonorus* Nymph (Edwards)

Dressing 4. Gold Ribbed Hare's Ear

Dressing 5. March Brown Nymph (Woolley)

Dressing 6. Flat-Body Nymph (Roberts)

Dressing 7. Klinken Nymph (Klinken)

Dressing 8. March Brown Nymph (Price)

5. March Brown Nymph (Woolley)

DRESSING

Hook length: Up to 15mm
Thread: Orange
Tail: Three brown mallard flank fibres
Abdomen: Brown fur
Rib: Gold wire
Thorax: Brown fur
Wingcase: Woodcock fibres over thorax area
Legs: Speckled grouse hackle fibres

6. Flat Body Nymph (Roberts)

DRESSING

Hook length: Up to 15mm
Thread: Olive
Tail: Brown partridge fibres
Abdomen: Olive-brown ostrich herl
Rib: Gold wire
Thorax: Dark-olive rabbit's fur picked out
Wingcase: Mottled brown fibres
Legs: Brown partridge fibres

7. Klinken Nymph (Klinken)

DRESSING

Hook length: Up to 15mm
Thread: Grey
Tail: Pheasant tail fibres
Abdomen: Olive-grey-brown ostrich herl
Rib: Olive swannundaze
Thorax: Grey squirrel
Wingcase: Pheasant tail fibres over thorax area
Legs: Tips of wingcase fibres turned under

8. March Brown Nymph (Price)

DRESSING

Hook length: Up to 15mm
Thread: Brown
Tail: Cock pheasant tail fibres
Abdomen: Hare's fur and antron
Rib: Gold wire
Thorax: As abdomen
Head/wingcase/back: Mottled turkey treated with varnish

The Laboured Swimmers

Leptophlebia, Paraleptophlebia, Habrophlebia (Plate 34)

This group includes two species of *Leptophlebia*: *Leptophlebia vespertina*, the Claret Dun and *Leptophlebia marginata*, the Sepia Dun; three species of *Paraleptophlebia*: *Paraleptophlebia submarginata*, the Turkey Brown, *Paraleptophlebia cincta*, the Purple Dun, and *Paraleptophlebia werneri*, which is rare and not covered in this book; and one species of *Habrophlebia*, *Habrophlebia fusca*, the Ditch Dun. These are rather attractive nymphs with long, slender gill filaments and long tails. They never move at anything more than a slow, steady swim. They are found in various habitats from stony streams to lakes, ponds and slow-flowing rivers. The nymphs are usually reddish-brown with long, feathery gills.

Plate 34

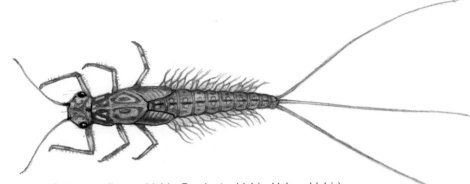

Laboured Swimmers (*Leptophlebia*, *Paraleptophlebia*, *Habrophlebia*)

Dressing 1. Claret Emerger (Price)

Dressing 2. Welsh Partridge (Williams)

Dressing 3. Sepia Nymph (Jacques)

Dressing 4. Mahogany Nymph (UK)

Dressing 5. Claret Nymph (Walker)

Dressing 6. Ditch Dun (Kite)

Dressing 7. Sepia Nymph (Walker)

Dressing 8. Claret Nymph (Henderson)

Dressings

1. Claret Emerger (Price)

DRESSING

Hook length: Up to 12mm
Thread: Claret
Tail: Cock pheasant tail fibres
Abdomen: Claret-brown fur dubbing
Rib: Gold wire
Thorax: Dark claret-brown fur
Emerging wing: Cul-de-canard feathers looped over thorax area

2. Welsh Partridge (Williams)

DRESSING

Hook length: Up to 12mm
Thread: Black
Tail: Brown partridge
Abdomen: Claret seal's fur sub
Rib: Oval gold
Legs: Brown partridge

3. Sepia Nymph (Jacques)

DRESSING

Hook length: Up to 12mm
Thread: Maroon
Tail: Red-brown cock hackle fibres well spaced
Abdomen: Cock pheasant tail fibres
Rib: Gold wire
Thorax: Black seal's fur sub
Wingcase: Cock pheasant fibres over thorax
Legs: Red hackle with a dark list

4. Mahogany Nymph (UK)

DRESSING

Hook length: Up to 12mm
Thread: Brown
Tail: Cock pheasant fibres
Abdomen: Mahogany coloured seal's fur sub
Rib: Brown pvc strip
Thorax: Mahogany seal's fur picked out
Wingcase: Partridge feather fibres

5. Claret Nymph (Walker)

DRESSING

Hook length: Up to 12mm
Thread: Brown
Tail: Black hen fibres long and spread out
Abdomen: Dark-brown seal's fur sub mixed with a small amount of ginger
Rib: Silver tinsel
Thorax: Black seal's fur sub
Wingcase: Black feather fibres
Legs: Dark-brown hen

6. Ditch Dun (Kite)

DRESSING

Hook length: Up to 12mm
Thread: Purple
Tail: White hackle fibres
Abdomen: Dark heron herls
Rib: Gold wire
Thorax: Dark heron herls
Legs: Blue-dun fibres under thorax

7. Sepia Nymph (Walker)

DRESSING

Hook length: Up to 12mm
Thread: Black
Tail: Dark hen pheasant fibres
Abdomen: Natural brown-black sheep's wool
Rib: Black plastic strip
Thorax: Black floss
Wingcase: Dark hen pheasant doubled over thorax
Legs: End of wingcase tied under

8. Claret Nymph (Henderson)

DRESSING

Hook length: Up to 12mm
Thread: Claret
Tail: Cock pheasant dyed claret
Abdomen: Cock pheasant dyed claret
Rib: Gold wire
Thorax: Dark-claret seal's fur sub
Hackle: Dark dun

The Agile Darters
Siphlonorus, Baetis, Centroptilum, Cloeon, Procloeon (Plates 35 and 36)

This is the largest of the groups and includes, by their habits and nature, some of the most important of the upwinged flies. *Siphlonorus* includes three species: *S. lacustris, alternatus* and *armatus*, all known under one common name, the Large Summer Dun. The *Baetis* group includes nine species: *B. niger muticus*, Iron Blue, *B. rhodani*, Large Dark Olive, *B. vernus* and *B. buceratus*, Medium Olive, *B. fuscatus*, Pale Watery, *B. scambus*, Small Dark Olive and *B. atrebatinus*, the Dark Olive Dun, and another species, *B. digitatus*, which is not covered in this book. The *Centroptilum*

include two species: *C. pennulatum*, Large Spurwing, and *C. luteolum*, the Small Spurwing. The *Cloeon* includes two species: *C. Simile*, the Lake Olive, and *C. dipterum*, the Pond Olive. Finally in this group is the one species of *Procloeon*: *P. bifidum*, the Pale Evening Dun.

The nymphs are all fairly similar and individual identification is very difficult in some cases. The nymphs of the *Siphlonorus* group are more obviously different, being fairly large and broad with overlapping large gill plates. The habitats in which the Agile Darters are found are very diverse, ranging from still waters to fast-flowing rivers, preferably with heavy weed growth. Most of the group are fairly slim and strong swimmers, but colouration varies between various shades of browns and greens. The sizes also cover a fairly wide range, from 8mm up to 18mm.

Dressings
1. Olive Emerger (Price)

DRESSING

Hook length: Up to 14mm
Thread: Olive
Tail: Cock pheasant fibres
Abdomen: Olive fur
Rib: Gold wire
Thorax: Dark-olive fur
Emerging wing: Cul-de-canard feathers over thorax

2. Olive Suspender Nymph

DRESSING

Hook length: Up to 14mm
Thread: Olive
Tail: Pale-olive cock fibres
Abdomen: Dirty-olive fur dubbing
Rib: Olive thread
Thorax: As abdomen
Suspender: Ethafoam ball in nylon mesh, coloured olive

Plate 35

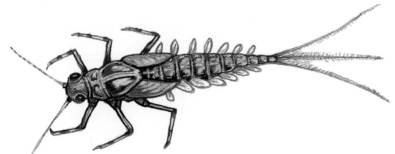

Agile Darters (*Baetis*, *Centroptilum*, *Cloeon*, *Procloeon*, *Siphlonorus*)

Dressing 1. Olive Emerger (Price)

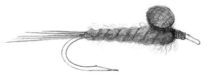

Dressing 2. Olive Suspender Nymph

Dressing 3. Emerger (Jardine)

Dressing 4. Olive Emerger

Dressing 5. Catskill Hendrickson (Steenrod)

Dressing 6. Olive Nymph (Collyer)

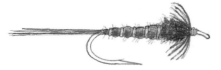

Dressing 7. Medium Olive Nymph (Skues)

Dressing 8. Olive Nymph

3. Emerger (Jardine)

DRESSING

Hook length: Up to 14mm
Thread: Crimson
Tails: Lemon wood duck
Abdomen: Olive-brown fur
Rib: Stripped quill
Thorax: Olive-brown fur
Emerging wings: Two small grey mallard feather slips
Legs: Lemon wood duck

4. Olive Emerger

DRESSING

Hook length: Up to 14mm
Thread: Brown
Tails: Pale-brown feather fibres
Abdomen: Olive fur
Rib: Gold wire
Thorax: Brown fur
Wingbuds: Two small pale-dun feather tips
Legs: Short olive cock

5. Catskill Hendrickson (Steenrod)

DRESSING

Hook length: Up to 14mm
Thread: Olive
Tails: Lemon wood duck fibres
Abdomen: Olive-grey fur
Rib: Gold wire
Thorax: Olive-grey fur
Wingcase: Grey goose
Legs: Brown partridge

6. Olive Nymph (Collyer)

DRESSING

Hook length: Up to 14mm
Thread: Olive
Tails: Olive goose fibres
Abdomen: Olive goose or olive heron herls
Rib: Oval gold tinsel
Thorax: Olive ostrich herl
Wingcase: Olive goose herl
Legs: Thorax picked out

7. Medium Olive Nymph (Skues)

DRESSING

Hook length: Up to 14mm
Thread: Primrose
Tails: Pale blue-dun cock
Abdomen: Olive heron herl
Rib: Gold wire
Thorax: Blue squirrel fur
Legs: Dark blue-dun cock

8 Olive Nymph

DRESSING

Hook length: Up to 14mm
Thread: Brown
Tails: Pheasant tail fibres
Abdomen: Olive seal's fur sub
Rib: Gold wire
Thorax: As abdomen
Wingcase: Grey goose or starling
Legs: Olive hen hackle

9. PVC Nymph (Goddard)

DRESSING

Hook length: Up to 14mm
Thread: Brown
Tails: Golden pheasant tips dyed olive
Abdomen: Olive heron herl
Rib: The abdomen is wrapped in overlapping turns of clear PVC strip
Thorax: Olive heron herl
Wingcase: Pheasant tail herl over thorax

10. Large Dark Olive Nymph (Price)

DRESSING

Hook length: Up to 14mm
Thread: Yellow
Tails: Dark olive fibres
Abdomen: Olive seal's fur sub and hare's ear
Rib: Gold wire
Thorax: Brown seal's fur sub
Wingcase: Dark-olive goose doubled over thorax
Legs: Olive cock fibres

11. Collyer's Brown Nymph (Collyer)

DRESSING

Hook length: Up to 14mm
Thread: Brown
Tails: Cock pheasant fibres
Abdomen: Cock pheasant fibres
Rib: Oval gold tinsel
Thorax: Chestnut-dyed ostrich herl
Wingcase: Cock pheasant fibres over thorax
Legs: Thorax picked out

12. GE Nymph (Jardine)

DRESSING

Hook length: Up to 14mm
Thread: Brown
Tails: Partridge breast fibres
Abdomen: Olive mole's fur
Rib: Copper wire
Thorax: Olive feather fibres
Wingcase: Back feather fibres
Legs: Thorax picked out

13. Large Dark Olive Nymph (Edwards)

DRESSING

Hook length: Up to 14mm
Thread: Dull orange
Tails: Medium olive badger hair
Abdomen: Olive-coloured polythene or flexibody in overlapping strips
Thorax: Olive-brown fur
Wingcase: Dark-brown turkey fibres either side of a strip of olive flexibody, tied in length of thorax
Legs: Speckled partridge tied lengthwise under wingcase

14. Pale Watery Nymph

DRESSING

Hook length: Up to 14mm
Thread: Yellow
Tails: Ginger cock fibres
Abdomen: Mixed cream and olive seal's fur sub
Thorax: Mixed cream and ginger seal's fur sub
Legs: Blue-dun hackle tied short

Plate 36

Dressing 9. PVC Nymph (Goddard)

Dressing 10. Large Dark Olive Nymph
(Price)

Dressing 11. Collyer's Brown Nymph
(Collyer)

Dressing 12. GE Nymph (Jardine)

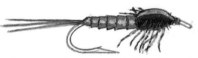

Dressing 13. Large Dark Olive Nymph
(Edwards)

Dressing 14. Pale Watery Nymph

Dressing 15. Iron Blue Nymph

Dressing 16. Iron Blue Nymph (Hidy)

Dressing 17. Spurwing Nymph
(Edwards)

Dressing 18. Spurwing Nymph
(Waites)

Dressing 19. Lake Olive Nymph
(Lane)

Dressing 20. Pond Olive Nymph
(Walker)

15. Iron Blue Nymph

DRESSING

Hook length: Up to 14mm
Thread: Claret
Tails: White cock fibres
Abdomen: Mole's fur with a tip of claret thread
Wingcase: Black feather fibres
Legs: Tips of wingcase fibres

16. Iron Blue Nymph (Hidy)

DRESSING

Hook length: Up to 14mm
Thread: Claret
Tails: Blue-dun fibres
Abdomen: Dubbed mole's fur
Thorax: As abdomen
Legs: Blue-dun hen hackle

17. Spurwing Nymph (Edwards)

DRESSING

Hook length: Up to 14mm
Thread: Spiderweb
Tails: Lemon wood duck fibres
Abdomen: Olive flexibody overlapping
Thorax: Olive dubbing
Wingbuds: Two strips of black feather fibres each side of thorax
Wingcase: Strip of olive flexibody over thorax area then brought forward and tied in at eye to form head
Legs: Grey partridge dyed yellow-olive lengthwise under wingbuds

18. Spurwing Nymph (Waites)

DRESSING

Hook length: Up to 14mm
Thread: Grey
Tails: Tips of heron herl
Abdomen: Natural heron herl
Rib: Silver fuse wire
Wingcase: Heron herl over thorax area

19. Lake Olive Nymph (Lane)

DRESSING

Hook length: Up to 14mm
Thread: Golden olive
Tail: Olive cock fibres
Abdomen: Olive silk
Rib: Gold wire
Thorax: As abdomen
Legs: Olive cock fibres under

20. Pond Olive Nymph (Walker)

DRESSING

Hook length: Up to 14mm
Thread: Yellow
Tail: Brown partridge fibres
Abdomen: Mix of ginger and brown seal's fur sub
Rib: Silver wire
Thorax: Brown seal's fur sub
Legs: Honey hen hackle

The Upwinged Fly Emergers

Emergers
(Plates 37 and 38)

The point of emergence in the fly life cycle is an important stage for the fly fisherman, as at this time the nymph swims to the surface to change into the dun and so becomes very vulnerable to trout. Not all upwinged species go through this stage – only those that hatch in open water; those that crawl out onto vegetation or rocks to change into the adult do not become available to the trout.

The emerger's wings are not yet fully open and the nymphal shuck is still attached to the abdomen of the emerging adult so the resulting fly is a merger of nymph and dun. In order to complete the emergence, the change from nymph to adult, the nymph swims up to the water surface or crawls out of the water. The wingcase begins to split along the top of the head making an opening through which the head and wings and forelegs can emerge. Once this has happened the dun has enough purchase to allow it to withdraw the abdomen. Now resting on the surface film, the fully formed dun takes a short time (depending on weather conditions) to dry its wings and take to the air. The nymphal skin is now an empty tube and floats away on the surface of the water.

Many different methods have been designed to make the artificial resemble the natural. All emerger patterns can be adapted to suit a particular species of natural fly by altering colours and sizes.

Dressings

1. Olive Loop-wing Emerger (Wolfle)

DRESSING

Hook length: Up to 14mm
Thread: Olive
Tail: Crinkled olive synthetic fibres
Abdomen: Brown-olive dubbing
Thorax: As abdomen but with a blue-dun hackle palmered over the area
Emerging wing: Same material as tail looped over thorax area

2. Hatching Nymph (Walker)

DRESSING

Hook length: Up to 14mm
Tail: Pale-olive fibres
Abdomen: Olive-brown fur
Thorax: As abdomen
Emerging wing: Polypropylene yarn
Legs: Olive-brown fibres

Plate 37

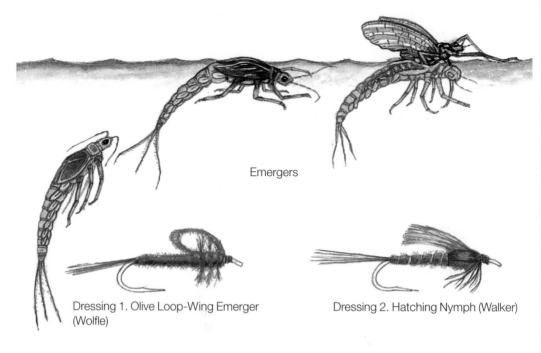

Emergers

Dressing 1. Olive Loop-Wing Emerger (Wolfle)

Dressing 2. Hatching Nymph (Walker)

Dressing 3. Emerger (Jardine)

Dressing 4. Muskrat Emerger (Jardine)

Dressing 5. Emerger (Swisher and Richards)

Dressing 6. Stillborn (Swisher and Richards)

Dressing 7. Pale Emerger (Price)

Dressing 8. Emerger (Jardine)

3. Emerger (Jardine)

DRESSING

Hook length: Up to 14mm
Thread: Crimson or to suit
Tail: Lemon wood duck fibres
Abdomen: Mix of mole and rabbit fur
Rib: Stripped quill
Emerging wing: Two small feather slips tied in either side of thorax
Legs: Lemon wood duck

4. Muskrat Emerger (Jardine)

DRESSING

Hook length: Up to 14mm
Thread: Brown
Tail: Honey hackle fibres
Abdomen: Muskrat fur
Thorax: As abdomen
Emerging wing: Cul-de-canard feathers looped over thorax area

5. Emerger (Swisher and Richards)

DRESSING

Hook length: Up to 14mm
Thread: Olive
Tail: Barred wood duck fibres
Abdomen: Olive-brown fur
Thorax: As abdomen
Emerging wing: Grey hen hackle tips
Legs: Wood duck fibres

6. Stillborn (Swisher and Richards)

DRESSING

Hook length: Up to 14mm
Thread: Olive
Tail: Hen hackle tip
Abdomen: Olive-brown fur or to suit natural
Wing: Feather fibres tied in flat over abdomen
Legs: Grey-brown feather fibres or to suit natural

7. Pale Emerger (Price)

DRESSING

Hook length: Up to 14mm
Thread: Yellow
Tail: Pheasant tail fibres
Abdomen: Pale-yellow dubbing
Rib: Gold wire
Thorax: As abdomen
Emerging wing: Cul-de-canard feathers over thorax area

8. Emerger (Jardine)

DRESSING

Hook length: Up to 14mm
Thread: Brown
Tail: Blue-dun hackle fibres
Abdomen: Olive-brown seal's fur sub
Emerging wing: Blue-dun hen hackle

9. Pheasant Tail Emerger (Klinken)

DRESSING

Hook length: Up to 14mm
Thread: Tan
Tail: Pheasant tail fibres
Abdomen: Pheasant tail fibres
Rib: Gold wire
Thorax: Peacock herl
Emerging wing: White polypropylene yarn
Hackle: Parachute red game hackle

10. Suspender Nymph (Goddard)

DRESSING

Hook length: Up to 14mm
Thread: Brown
Tail: Greenwell hackle fibres
Abdomen: Goose fibres dyed olive
Rib: Gold wire
Thorax: Dark-olive seal's fur sub
Wingcase: Brown feather fibres and small ethafoam ball in ladies tights material
Legs: Tips of wingcase turned under

11. Yellow May Dun Emerger (Edwards)

DRESSING

Hook length: 14mm
Thread: Yellow
Tail: Grey partridge fibres dyed sulphur yellow
Abdomen: Fur dyed sulphur yellow
Rib: Overlapping turns of clear polythene strip to cover abdomen
Thorax: As abdomen
Wingcase: Grey partridge fibres dyed sulphur yellow over thorax area
Emerging wing: Light-brown raffene shape as small wings either side of front half of abdomen
Legs: Grey partridge fibres dyed sulphur yellow, feather tied in lengthways under thorax area

12. Emerger (Jardine)

DRESSING

Hook length: Up to 14mm
Thread: Brown
Tail: Wood duck fibres
Abdomen: Dark-olive antron
Rib: Fibres of white string
Thorax: As abdomen
Emerging wing: Pale-grey antron
Legs: Parachute golden-olive cock

13. Iron Blue Emerger (Lawrie)

DRESSING

Hook length: Up to 14mm
Thread: Claret
Tail: Cream hen fibres
Abdomen: Dubbed mole fur
Thorax: Fur dyed dark blue-purple
Emerging wing: Pale slate-blue cock, lower fibres cut away
Legs: Dark grey-blue cock, upper fibres removed

14. Hare's Ear Emerger (Price)

DRESSING

Hook length: Up to 14mm
Thread: Brown
Tail: Cock pheasant tail fibres
Abdomen: Hare's ear
Rib: Gold wire
Thorax: As abdomen
Emerging wing: Cul-de-canard over thorax area

Plate 38

Dressing 9. Pheasant Tail Emerger
(Klinken)

Dressing 10. Suspender Nymph
(Goddard)

Dressing 11. Yellow May Dun Emerger
(Edwards)

Dressing 12. Emerger (Jardine)

Dressing 13. Iron Blue Emerger (Lawrie)

Dressing 14. Hare's Ear Emerger (Price)

Dressing 15. Stillborn Emerger
(Swisher and Richards)

Dressing 16. Hatching Olive (Goddard)

Dressing 17. Tup's Emerger (Price)

Dressing 18. March Brown Emerger
(Jardine)

Dressing 19. Mayfly Emerger (Price)

Dressing 20. Hatching Olive (Bucknall)

15. Stillborn Emerger (Swisher and Richards)

DRESSING

Hook length: Up to 14mm
Thread: Brown
Tail: Hackle divided at the rear to form two tails, the other fibres pulled forwards and tied in golden-olive
Abdomen: Olive-brown fur
Thorax: Brown fur
Emerging wing: Two small grey feather slips

16. Hatching Olive (Goddard)

DRESSING

Hook length: Up to 14mm
Thread: Brown
Tail: Green-olive herls (condor sub)
Abdomen: Olive-green herls
Rib: Silver lurex. The abdomen and rib are then covered with olive PVC
Thorax: Cock pheasant fibres
Legs: Honey hen hackle

17. Tup's Emerger (Price)

DRESSING

Hook length: Up to 14mm
Thread: Yellow
Tail: Cock pheasant tail fibres
Abdomen: Cream-yellow fur
Rib: Gold wire
Thorax: Pinkish-coloured dubbing
Emerging wing: Cul-de-canard feathers over thorax area

18. March Brown Emerger (Jardine)

DRESSING

Hook length: Up to 14mm
Thread: Brown
Tail: Deer hair
Abdomen: Dubbed deer hair
Rib: Gold wire
Thorax: Deer hair picked out
Emerging wing: Antron floss

19. Mayfly Emerger (Price)

DRESSING

Hook length: Up to 18mm
Thread: Brown
Tail: Cock pheasant fibres
Abdomen: Yellow-cream dubbing
Rib: Brown thread
Thorax: Olive-yellow dubbing
Emerging wing: Cul-de-canard feathers over thorax area

20. Hatching Olive (Bucknall)

DRESSING

Hook length: Up to 14mm
Thread: Olive
Tail: Goose dyed olive or olive feather fibres
Abdomen: Pale-olive dyed goose herls
Rib: Gold tinsel
Thorax: Olive dubbing
Wingcase: Dark olive-brown feather fibres over thorax
Legs: Small brown hen hackle

The Upwinged Fly Spinners

Spinners (Imago Stage)

After the nymph has changed into the dun (the subimago) it will find a resting place amongst trees or bankside vegetation where it can change into the spinner (the imago) stage. Just as in the emergence from nymph to dun, the upper thorax and head area split to allow an opening through which the imago's head, legs and thorax can emerge. Once the legs can find some form of purchase the wings and abdomen can be drawn free from the now discarded skin of the dun. Moulting times vary from species to species: the tiny *caenis* goes through this stage in a very short time but some of the other upwinged flies may remain duns for up to three days. A major transformation has now taken place, with the rather drab colours of the dun and the dull wings giving way to a brighter, and in some species, differently coloured fly with transparent, shiny wings.

In the spinner stage the fly can carry out its most important task – to mate. Mating takes place in flight with the male holding the female from below, bending the front legs over her thorax and using his claspers to hold the abdomen. They continue to fly in this manner, slowly descending earthwards until copulation is complete, which takes only a very short time. Before reaching the ground the mated pair now separate and the female makes her way back to the water to lay her eggs. Soon after egg-laying is completed the female usually falls onto the water surface and dies.

Because of the differences in species some flies are very important to the fisherman in the spinner stages, whereas others are of doubtful value and some are of no interest at all. The spinners illustrated are all, to some degree, of interest to the fly fisherman and are shown along with the patterns designed to represent them. All the spinners shown are female, the differences between male and female being given in the individual species chapters.

The Autumn Dun
(*Ecdyonorus dispar*)
(Plate 39)
Large Red Spinner, Autumn Spinner

Natural

Size:	Up to 13mm
Tails:	Red-brown
Abdomen:	Rich red-brown
Wings:	Clear, shiny with brown veins
Legs:	Olive-brown
Eyes:	Red-brown
Remarks:	Male of no interest. Female spinner lands on a suitable stone protruding from the water surface and dips her abdomen into the water to release her eggs

Dressings

1. Autumn Spinner

DRESSING

Hook length: Up to 13mm
Thread: Red-brown
Tail: Brown microfibetts
Abdomen: Red-brown seal's fur sub
Rib: Gold wire
Wing: Pale-brown partridge

2. Great Red Spinner (Harris)

DRESSING

Hook length: Up to 13mm
Thread: Claret
Tail: Dark rusty-dun fibres
Abdomen: Dark-red seal's fur sub
Rib: Gold wire
Wing: Dark rusty-dun cock with upper and lower fibres cut away

The Blue-Winged Olive
(*Ephemerella ignita*)
(Plate 39)
Sherry Spinner

Natural

Size:	Up to 10mm
Tails:	Pale grey
Abdomen:	Orange-brown
Wings:	Bright, clear with pale yellow-brown veins
Legs:	Pale orange-brown
Eyes:	Dark olive
Remarks:	Both male and female spinner are of interest; the female flies down to the water surface to release her eggs

Dressings

3. Sherry Spinner (Lunn)

DRESSING

Hook length: Up to 10mm
Thread: Pale orange
Tail: Pale-ginger cock fibres
Abdomen: Hackle stalk dyed orange or orange-brown floss
Wing: Pale blue-dun hackle tips spent position
Hackle: Red game cock

4. Sherry Spinner (Conba)

DRESSING

Hook length: Up to 10mm
Thread: Orange-brown
Tail: Pale-ginger cock
Abdomen: Orange-brown seal's fur sub
Wing: Antron tied spent

Plate 39

Spinners: Autumn Dun, Blue-Winged Olive, *Caenis*

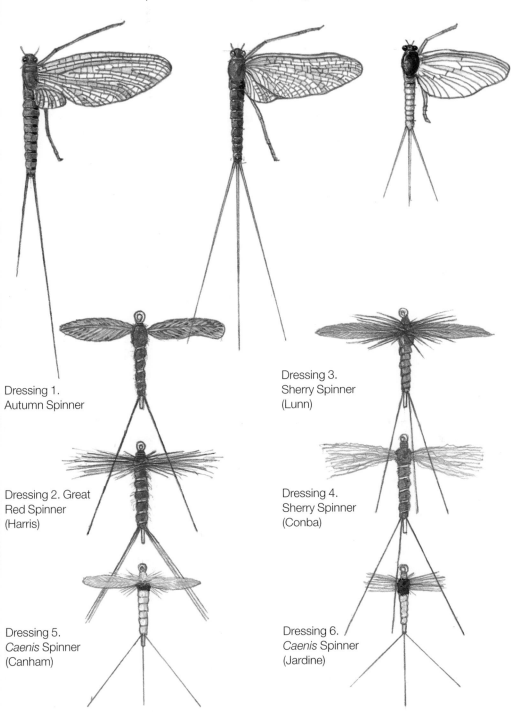

Dressing 1.
Autumn Spinner

Dressing 2. Great
Red Spinner
(Harris)

Dressing 5.
Caenis Spinner
(Canham)

Dressing 3.
Sherry Spinner
(Lunn)

Dressing 4.
Sherry Spinner
(Conba)

Dressing 6.
Caenis Spinner
(Jardine)

Caenis

(*Caenis* and *Brachycercus* species) (Plate 39)
Caenis Spinner

Natural

Size:	Up to 5mm
Tails:	White
Abdomen:	Cream, with brown thorax area
Wings:	Bright, clear
Legs:	Pale grey
Eyes:	Dark brown
Remarks:	Both male and female spinners are of interest; the female flies down to water surface to release her eggs

Dressings

5. Caenis Spinner (Canham)

DRESSING

Hook length: Up to 5mm
Thread: White midge
Tail: White cock fibres
Abdomen: White polythene in overlapping turns
Thorax: Brown turkey herl
Wing: Very small white feather tips, spent
Hackle: Very short white cock trimmed bottom side only

6. Caenis Spinner (Jardine)

DRESSING

Hook length: Up to 5mm
Thread: White midge
Tail: White microfibetts
Abdomen: Cream rabbit's fur
Thorax: Brown rabbit's fur
Hackle: White cock trimmed top and bottom

The Claret Dun

(*Leptophlebia vespertina*) (Plate 40)
Claret Spinner

Natural

Size:	Up to 10mm
Tails:	Pale brown
Abdomen:	Rich dark brown
Wings:	Bright, clear with light-brown veins
Legs:	Pale brown
Eyes:	Dark red-brown
Remarks:	Male of no interest; female flies down to water surface to release her eggs

Dressings

1. Claret Spinner

DRESSING

Hook length: Up to 10mm
Thread: Black
Tail: Honey dun fibres
Abdomen: Dark red-brown seal's fur
Rib: Gold wire
Hackle: Honey dun tied in two bunches to represent spent wings

2. Claret Spinner (Harris)

DRESSING

Hook length: Up to 10mm
Thread: Claret
Tail: Blue-dun cock fibres
Abdomen: Claret seal's fur
Hackle: Blue-dun clipped top and bottom to have spent wings

The Dusky Yellowstreak

(Heptagenia lateralis)
(Plate 40)
Dusky Yellowstreak Spinner

Natural

Size:	Up to 10mm
Tails:	Pale brown
Abdomen:	Amber-brown, with two yellow stripes either side of thorax area
Wings:	Bright, clear with brown veins
Legs:	Olive-brown
Eyes:	Brown-black
Remarks:	The female flies down to water surface to release her eggs

Dressings

3. Pheasant Tail Spinner

DRESSING

Hook length: Up to 10mm
Thread: Brown
Tail: Blue-dun cock fibres
Abdomen: Cock pheasant tail fibres
Wing: Blue-dun cock hackle tips tied in spent
Hackle: Golden dun cock

4. Dusky Yellowstreak Spinner

DRESSING

Hook length: Up to 10mm
Thread: Brown
Tail: Red game fibres
Abdomen: Olive-brown seal's fur, last third orange-brown
Rib: Gold wire
Hackle: Pale red-brown cock tied into two bunches, spent

The Iron Blue

(Baetis niger, muticus)
(Plate 40)
Little Claret Spinner (female), Jenny Spinner (male)

Natural

Size:	Up to 7mm
Tails:	Pale olive-grey
Abdomen:	Claret-brown
Wings:	Bright, transparent
Legs:	Pale olive-grey
Eyes:	Red-brown
Remarks:	Male not as important as female. Female spinner is thought to go under water to lay her eggs, her body then floating to the surface. This would make the fly very low-riding due to the surface film

Dressings

5. Houghton Ruby (Lunn)

DRESSING

Hook length: Up to 7mm
Thread: Crimson
Tail: White cock fibres
Abdomen: Red game hackle stalk dyed crimson
Wing: Pale blue-dun hackle tips, spent
Hackle: Red game

6. Iron Blue Spinner (Walker)

DRESSING

Hook length: Up to 7mm
Thread: Crimson
Tail: Fine white hairs
Abdomen: Magenta and chestnut wool mixed 1:2
Rib: Crimson thread
Thorax: Sepia wool
Wing: Two spent bunches of fine hair dyed slate grey

Plate 40

Spinners: Claret Dun, Dusky Yellowstreak, Iron Blue

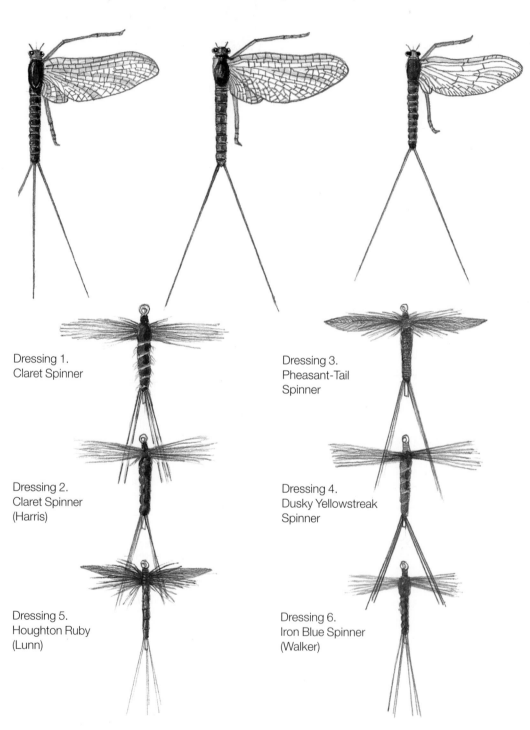

Dressing 1.
Claret Spinner

Dressing 2.
Claret Spinner
(Harris)

Dressing 5.
Houghton Ruby
(Lunn)

Dressing 3.
Pheasant-Tail
Spinner

Dressing 4.
Dusky Yellowstreak
Spinner

Dressing 6.
Iron Blue Spinner
(Walker)

Lake Olive

(*Cloeon simile*) (Plate 41)
Lake Olive Spinner

Natural

Size:	Up to 9mm
Tails:	Cream
Abdomen:	Red-brown tending to olive-brown under
Wings:	Bright, transparent with a tinge of yellow
Legs:	Olive
Eyes:	Olive-green
Remarks:	Male of limited interest; female flies down to water surface to release her eggs

Dressings

1. Lake Olive Spinner (Walker)

> **DRESSING**
>
> **Hook length**: Up to 10mm
> **Thread**: Black
> **Tail**: Blue-dun fibres
> **Abdomen**: Dark-red seal's fur
> **Rib**: Gold tinsel
> **Wing**: Blue-dun, preferably with a yellow tinge

2. Lake Olive Spinner (Harris)

> **DRESSING**
>
> **Hook length**: Up to 10mm
> **Thread**: Orange
> **Tail**: Rusty-dun fibres
> **Abdomen**: Dark red-brown seal's fur
> **Rib**: Gold wire
> **Wing**: Pale grizzle fibres bunched and tied spent

Large Brook Dun

(*Ecdyonorus torrentis*)
(Plate 41) Large Red Spinner

Natural

Size:	Up to 14mm
Tails:	Red-brown
Abdomen:	Red-brown with darker diagonal bands along sides
Wings:	Bright, transparent brown veins
Legs:	Olive, red-brown
Eyes:	Red-brown
Remarks:	Male and female both of interest; female flies down to water surface to release her eggs

Dressings

3. Great Red Spinner (Woolley)

> **DRESSING**
>
> **Hook length**: Up to 14mm
> **Thread**: Dark red
> **Tail**: Red game cock fibres
> **Abdomen**: Dark-red seal's fur
> **Rib**: Gold wire
> **Wings**: Two bunches of blue-dun hackle fibres tied spent
> **Hackle**: Red game cock

4. Pheasant Tail Spinner (Collier)

> **DRESSING**
>
> **Hook length**: Up to 14mm
> **Thread**: Dark red
> **Tail**: Honey-dun fibres
> **Abdomen**: Pheasant tail fibres
> **Rib**: Gold wire
> **Hackle**: Honey-dun trimmed top and bottom

117

Plate 41

Spinners: Lake Olive, Large Brook Dun, Large Spurwing

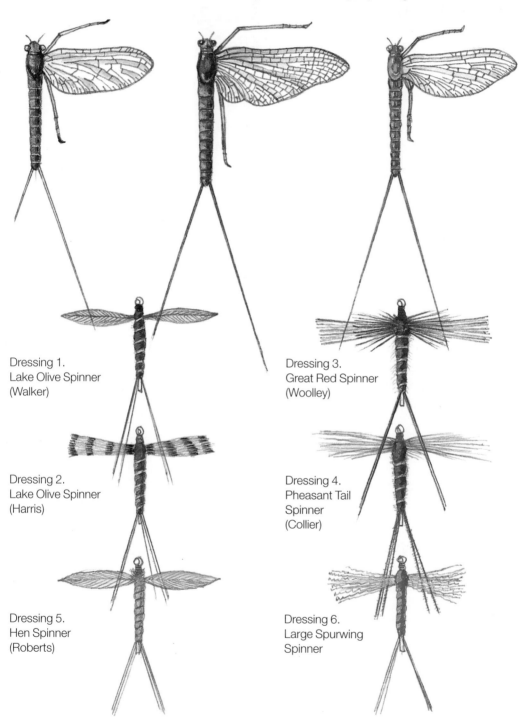

Dressing 1.
Lake Olive Spinner
(Walker)

Dressing 2.
Lake Olive Spinner
(Harris)

Dressing 5.
Hen Spinner
(Roberts)

Dressing 3.
Great Red Spinner
(Woolley)

Dressing 4.
Pheasant Tail
Spinner
(Collier)

Dressing 6.
Large Spurwing
Spinner

Large Spurwing
(*Centroptilum pennulatum*)
(Plate 41)
Large Amber Spinner

Natural
Size:	Up to 10mm
Tails:	Pale grey
Abdomen:	Amber with pale-amber segmentation
Wings:	Bright, transparent
Legs:	Olive
Eyes:	Pale olive
Remarks:	Male of limited interest; female spinner flies down to water surface to release her eggs

Dressings

5. Hen Spinner (Roberts)

DRESSING

Hook length: Up to 10mm
Thread: Orange
Tail: Cream cock fibres
Abdomen: A mix of olive, white and amber seal's fur sub
Wing: Spent hen hackle tips cream coloured

6. Large Spurwing Spinner

DRESSING

Hook length: Up to 10mm
Thread: Orange-brown
Tail: Grey feather fibres
Abdomen: Amber seal's fur sub
Wing: White polypropylene yarn tied spent

Large Summer Dun
(*Siphlonorus lacustris*)
(Plate 42)
Great Red Spinner

Natural
Size:	Up to 15mm
Tails:	Dark olive
Abdomen:	Green-brown
Wings:	Transparent with brown veins
Legs:	Dark olive
Eyes:	Red-brown
Remarks:	Males and females can become available to trout; female flies down to water surface to release her eggs

Dressings

1. Large Summer Spinner (Price)

DRESSING

Hook length: Up to 14mm
Thread: Red-brown
Tail: Dark-olive fibres
Abdomen: Brown polypropylene
Rib: Yellow
Wing: Pale-brown partridge tied spent

2. Summer Spinner

DRESSING

Hook length: Up to 14mm
Thread: Red-brown
Tail: Brown fibres
Abdomen: Olive-brown seal's fur
Rib: Gold thread
Wing: Pale-brown feather tips
Hackle: Short ginger clipped top and bottom

119

Plate 42

Spinners: Large Summer Dun, Late March Brown

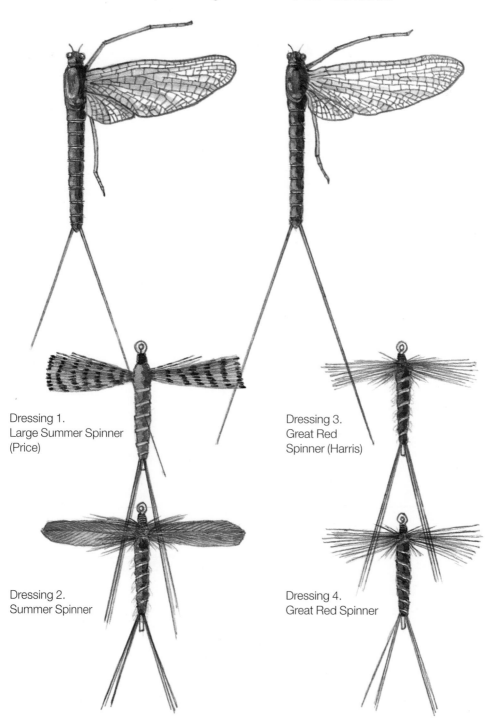

Dressing 1.
Large Summer Spinner
(Price)

Dressing 3.
Great Red
Spinner (Harris)

Dressing 2.
Summer Spinner

Dressing 4.
Great Red Spinner

Late March Brown
(*Ecdyonorus venosus*) (Plate 42)
Great Red Spinner

Natural

Size: Up to 14mm
Tails: Brown
Abdomen: Rich red-brown
Wings: Transparent with pale-brown veins
Legs: Pale brown
Eyes: Dark brown
Remarks: Both male and female can become available to the trout but in very limited numbers; female flies down to water surface to release her eggs

Dressings

3. Great Red Spinner (Harris)

> **DRESSING**
>
> **Hook length:** Up to 14mm
> **Thread:** Claret
> **Tail:** Rusty-dun fibres
> **Abdomen:** Dark claret-red seal's fur sub
> **Rib:** Gold wire
> **Hackle:** Rusty-dun cock, a 'V' cut out top and bottom

4. Great Red Spinner

> **DRESSING**
>
> **Hook length:** Up to 14mm
> **Thread:** Brown
> **Tail:** Ginger cock fibres
> **Abdomen:** Rich claret pheasant tail fibres
> **Rib:** Gold thread
> **Hackle:** Pale-ginger cock fibres bunched to give spent wings

Mayfly
(*Ephemera danica, vulgata, lineata*) (Plate 43)
Spent Gnat, Grey Drake, Black Drake (male)

Natural

Size: Up to 20mm
Tails: Dark brown
Abdomen: Creamy white, last three segments have brown, triangular markings
Wings: Bright, transparent with obvious veins and small, dark areas
Legs: Olive
Eyes: Olive-black
Remarks: The female and some males end up on the water in great numbers in a good season; the female flies down to the water surface to release her eggs

Dressings

1. Plastazote Mayfly (Kendall)

> **DRESSING**
>
> **Hook length:** Up to 20mm
> **Thread:** Dark brown
> **Tail:** Cock pheasant fibres
> **Abdomen:** Plastazote strip in overlapping turns
> **Rib:** Brown floss
> **Wing:** Teal feathers tied in spent
> **Hackle:** Brown cock

Plate 43

Spinners: Mayfly

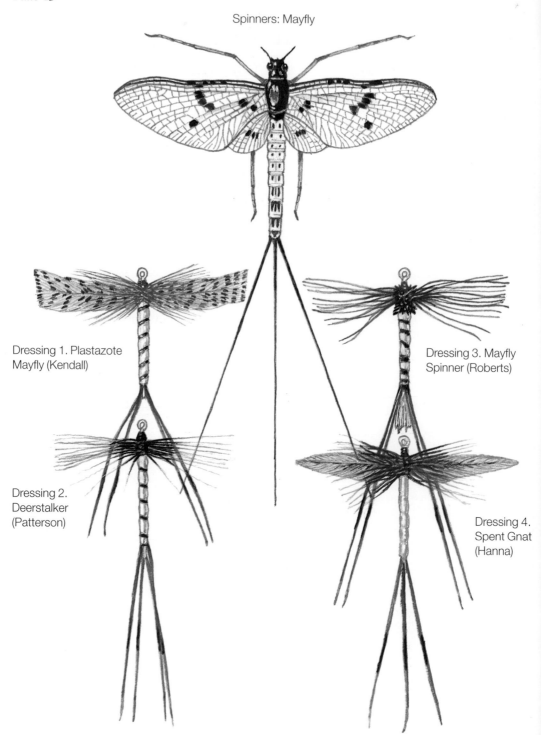

Dressing 1. Plastazote
Mayfly (Kendall)

Dressing 3. Mayfly
Spinner (Roberts)

Dressing 2.
Deerstalker
(Patterson)

Dressing 4.
Spent Gnat
(Hanna)

2. Deerstalker (Patterson)

DRESSING

Hook length: Up to 20mm
Thread: Brown
Tail: Pheasant tail fibres long
Abdomen: White-cream deer hair running from thorax to bend and protruding
Rib: Brown thread and silver wire
Hackle: Brown cock and black cock; the black fibres cover thorax area and are cut very short, the brown fibres are bunched to form spent wings

3. Mayfly Spinner (Roberts)

DRESSING

Hook length: Up to 20mm
Thread: Black
Tail: Pheasant tail fibres
Abdomen: White floss silk
Rib: Black thread
Hackle: Badger cock tied in spent

4. Spent Gnat (Hanna)

DRESSING

Hook length: Up to 20mm
Thread: Black
Tail: Cock pheasant tail fibres
Abdomen: White translucent plastic in strips bound over the hook, built up to make shape of body
Wings: Blue-dun hackle points spent
Hackle: Badger cock

Medium Olive

(*Baetis vernus*) (Plate 44)
Red Spinner, Medium Olive Spinner

Natural

Size:	Up to 9mm
Tails:	Pale grey
Abdomen:	Rich red-brown
Wings:	Transparent with pale brown veins
Legs:	Grey-brown
Eyes:	Brown
Remarks:	Male and female spinners become available to the trout, the female more important. She goes underwater to lay her eggs, her spent body then returns to surface. The artificial should be in the surface film

Dressings
1. Lunn's Particular (Lunn)

DRESSING

Hook length: Up to 9mm
Thread: Crimson
Tail: Red game fibres
Abdomen: Rhode Island red hackle stalk
Wing: Blue-dun hackle tips
Hackle: Red game, top/bottom fibres removed

2. USD Poly-Spinner (Goddard and Clarke)

DRESSING

Hook length: Up to 9mm
Thread: Brown
Tail: Well-spaced Magic Spinner fibres
Abdomen: Rusty-red polypropylene dubbing
Wing: Polythene pierced with a needle to get some surface pattern
Hackle: Red game, top/bottom fibres removed or tied on upside down in parachute style

123

Plate 44

Spinners: Medium Olive, Olive Upright, Pale Evening Dun

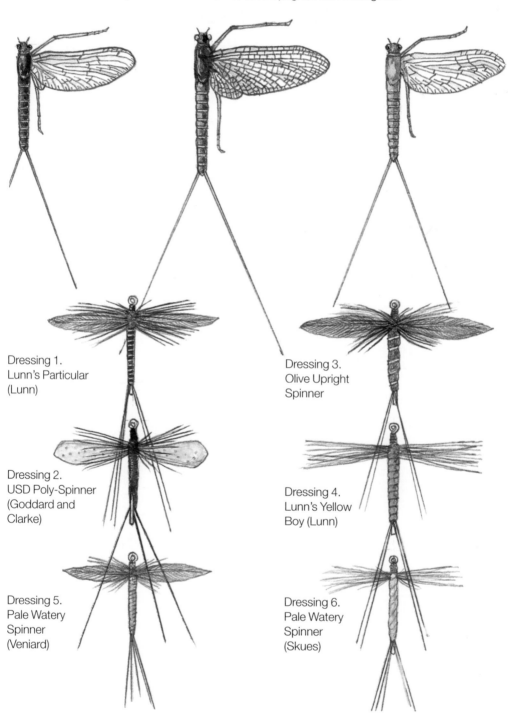

Dressing 1.
Lunn's Particular
(Lunn)

Dressing 2.
USD Poly-Spinner
(Goddard and
Clarke)

Dressing 5.
Pale Watery
Spinner
(Veniard)

Dressing 3.
Olive Upright
Spinner

Dressing 4.
Lunn's Yellow
Boy (Lunn)

Dressing 6.
Pale Watery
Spinner
(Skues)

Olive Upright

(*Rhithrogena semicolorata*)
(Plate 44)
Yellow Upright

Natural

Size:	Up to 12mm
Tails:	Pale olive-grey
Abdomen:	Olive-brown with paler banding
Wings:	Transparent with pale-brown veins
Legs:	Pale olive
Eyes:	Pale olive
Remarks:	Both male and female spinners become available to trout, the female more important. She flies down to rocks or vegetation protruding from water surface and dips her abdomen into water to release eggs

Dressings

3. Olive Upright Spinner

DRESSING

Hook length: Up to 12mm
Thread: Olive
Tail: Pale blue-dun fibres
Abdomen: Olive-brown seal's fur sub
Rib: Gold thread
Wings: Blue-dun tips spent
Hackle: Red game clipped flat top and bottom

4. Lunn's Yellow Boy (Lunn)

DRESSING

Hook length: Up to 12mm
Thread: Pale orange
Tail: Buff cock fibres
Abdomen: Hackle stalk dyed olive-brown or similar-coloured seal's fur
Wing: Pale-buff cock tied spent

Pale Evening Dun

(*Procloeon bifidum*)
(Plate 44) Golden Spinner,
Pale Evening Spinner

Natural

Size:	Up to 7mm
Tails:	Pale yellow
Abdomen:	Rich yellow
Wings:	Bright, clear with a tinge of green to front edge
Legs:	Pale yellow
Eyes:	Brown
Remarks:	Both male and female are of little value. The female is said to fly down to the water surface to release her eggs, mostly after dusk

Dressings

5. Pale Watery Spinner (Veniard)

DRESSING

Hook length: Up to 7mm
Thread: Pale yellow
Tail: Golden-yellow fibres
Abdomen: Pale-yellow thread covered with natural horsehair
Wing: Very pale blue-dun tips tied spent
Hackle: Pale-golden yellow cock

6. Pale Watery Spinner (Skues)

DRESSING

Hook length: Up to 7mm
Thread: Pale orange
Tail: Honey-dun fibres
Abdomen: Creamy-yellow wool
Hackle: Pale blue-dun fibres bunched and tied spent

Pale Watery

(*Baetis fuscatus*) (Plate 45)
Golden Spinner, Pale Watery Spinner

Natural

Size: Up to 7mm
Tails: Pale grey
Abdomen: Golden-olive
Wings: Bright, clear
Legs: Pale olive
Eyes: Red-brown
Remarks: Males are of little interest. The female returns to water late in the day and crawls under the surface to lay her eggs, her spent body then becoming trapped in surface film

Dressings

1. Tup's Indispensable (Austin)

> **DRESSING**
>
> **Hook length**: Up to 7mm
> **Thread**: Yellow
> **Tail**: Pale blue-dun fibres
> **Abdomen**: Modern: rear half yellow floss, front half a mix of yellow, red and honey seal's fur. Original: tip of yellow silk, the rest a mix of ram's testicle fur, lemon fur from a spaniel, cream and crimson seal's fur
> **Hackle**: Pale blue-dun or honey-dun tied spent

2. Pale Watery Spinner (Warrilow)

> **DRESSING**
>
> **Hook length**: Up to 7mm
> **Thread**: Cream
> **Tail**: Honey fibres
> **Abdomen**: Stripped yellow hackle stalk
> **Thorax**: Ginger antron
> **Wing**: Cream yarn tied spent

Pond Olive

(*Cloeon dipterum*) (Plate 45)
Apricot Spinner, Pond Olive Spinner

Natural

Size: Up to 9mm
Tail: Brown
Abdomen: Apricot
Wings: Transparent with pale-bronze leading edge
Legs: Olive
Eyes: Pale olive-green
Remarks: Male is of little importance. Swarming takes place in the evening so the spinners are mostly available at night or early morning. The female is the only species in Britain that is oviparous – the eggs hatch immediately on contact with water

Dressings

3. Pond Olive Spinner (Goddard)

> **DRESSING**
>
> **Hook length**: Up to 9mm
> **Thread**: Orange
> **Tail**: Pale badger cock fibres
> **Abdomen**: Goose herl dyed apricot then covered with overlapping turns of pale-olive PVC
> **Wings**: Pale blue-dun feather tips spent
> **Hackle**: Honey-dun fibres tied in two bunches under the wings

Plate 45

Spinners: Pale Watery, Pond Olive, Small Dark Olive

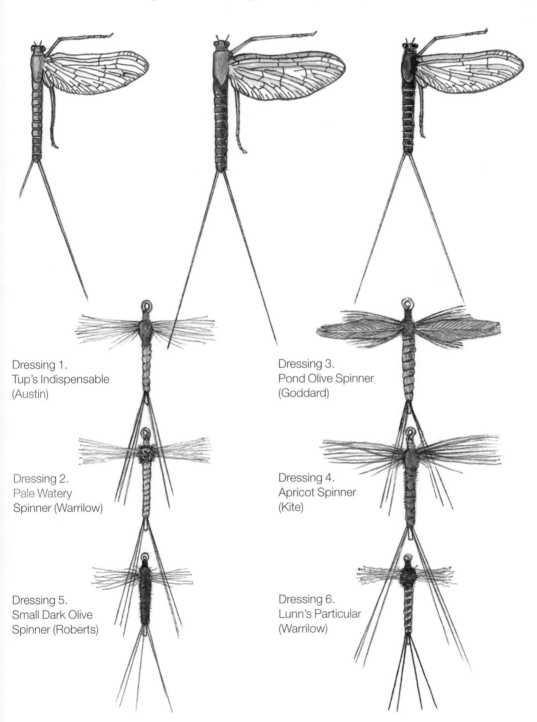

Dressing 1.
Tup's Indispensable
(Austin)

Dressing 2.
Pale Watery
Spinner (Warrilow)

Dressing 5.
Small Dark Olive
Spinner (Roberts)

Dressing 3.
Pond Olive Spinner
(Goddard)

Dressing 4.
Apricot Spinner
(Kite)

Dressing 6.
Lunn's Particular
(Warrilow)

4. Apricot Spinner (Kite)

DRESSING

Hook length: Up to 9mm
Thread: Golden-olive
Tail: Honey-dun fibres
Abdomen: Swan herls dyed apricot
Hackle: Pale honey dun tied in bunches, spent

Small Dark Olive

(*Baetis scambus*) (Plate 45) Small Dark Olive Spinner, Small Red Spinner

Natural

Size:	Up to 6mm
Tails:	Grey
Abdomen:	Rich brown
Wings:	Clear with dark-grey veins
Legs:	Brown
Eyes:	Black
Remarks:	Males are of some interest but the female is very important. The female goes underwater, crawling down protruding objects, to lay her eggs. She then floats to the surface where, trapped in the surface film, she is an easy meal for the watchful trout

Dressings

5. Small Dark Olive Spinner (Roberts)

DRESSING

Hook length: Up to 6mm
Thread: Brown
Tail: Blue-dun fibres
Abdomen: Rust-red seal's fur sub
Wing: Pale blue-dun bunched and tied spent

6. Lunn's Particular (Warrilow)

DRESSING

Hook length: Up to 6mm
Thread: Crimson
Tail: Rhode Island Red fibres
Abdomen: Stripped hackle stalk wound on
Thorax: Rich-brown antron
Wing: Cream poly yarn

Small Spurwing
(*Centroptilum luteolum*)
(Plate 46)
Little Amber Spinner, Small Spurwing Spinner

Natural

Size:	Up to 7mm
Tails:	Grey-olive
Abdomen:	Yellow-brown with pale segmentation
Wings:	Bright, transparent with a hint of olive
Legs:	Pale olive
Eyes:	Dark olive
Remarks:	Male and female are of interest. The female lays her eggs by flying down to the water surface

Dressings

1. Tup's Para (Russell)

DRESSING

Hook length: Up to 7mm
Thread: Yellow
Tail: Cream cock fibres
Abdomen: Yellow floss
Thorax: A mix of pink, orange and yellow dubbing
Hackle: Cream cock tied parachute

2. Lunn's Yellow Boy (Lunn)

DRESSING

Hook length: Up to 7mm
Thread: Pale orange
Tail: Pale-buff cock fibres
Abdomen: Hackle stalk dyed medium yellow
Wing: Buff hackle tips spent
Hackle: Pale buff, top/bottom fibres removed

Yellow Evening Dun
(*Ephemerella notata*)
(Plate 46)
Yellow Evening Spinner

Natural

Size:	Up to 10mm
Tail:	Olive
Abdomen:	Yellow
Wings:	Bright, transparent with yellow tinge to leading edge
Legs:	Yellow
Eyes:	Green
Remarks:	Very localized species and of limited interest from a fishing point of view. Swarming is said to take place at dusk so most spinners would be available at night or early morning. The female flies down to water surface to release her eggs

Dressings

3. Yellow Evening Spinner (Harris)

DRESSING

Hook length: Up to 10mm
Thread: Orange
Tail: Cream cock fibres
Abdomen: Pale-yellow seal's fur with a tip of orange thread
Wing: Honey cock fibres tied in spent

Plate 46

Spinners: Small Spurwing, Yellow Evening Dun, Yellow May Dun

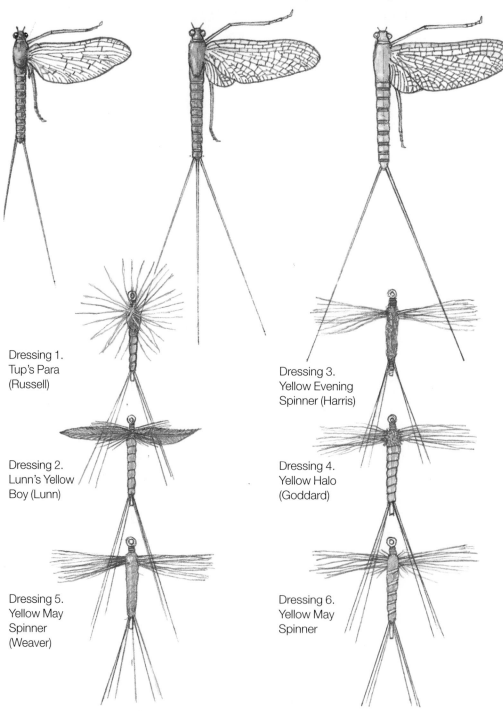

Dressing 1.
Tup's Para
(Russell)

Dressing 3.
Yellow Evening
Spinner (Harris)

Dressing 2.
Lunn's Yellow
Boy (Lunn)

Dressing 4.
Yellow Halo
(Goddard)

Dressing 5.
Yellow May
Spinner
(Weaver)

Dressing 6.
Yellow May
Spinner

4. Yellow Halo (Goddard)

DRESSING

Hook length: Up to 10mm
Thread: Yellow
Tail: Honey-dun fibres
Abdomen: Cream goose herls covered with overlapping strips of yellow plastic
Thorax: Yellow cock hackle trimmed very short
Hackle: Cream cock fibres removed top and bottom

Yellow May Dun
(*Heptagenia sulphurea*)
(Plate 46)
Yellow May Spinner

Natural

Size:	Up to 12mm
Tail:	Grey
Abdomen:	Golden yellow
Wings:	Transparent with pale-yellow leading edge
Legs:	Pale olive
Eyes:	Pale blue
Remarks:	Of little interest from a fishing point of view apart from the rivers where it occurs in sufficient numbers to arouse the trout. Because swarming takes place late in the day the returning female lays her eggs on the water surface towards evening, and is therefore of limited interest

Dressings

5. Yellow May Spinner (Weaver)

DRESSING

Hook length: Up to 12mm
Thread: Cream
Tail: Golden-yellow antron wool
Abdomen: Golden-yellow SLF
Wings: Deer hair colour of honey dun, tied spent

6. Yellow May Spinner

DRESSING

Hook length: Up to 12mm
Thread: Yellow
Tail: Yellow cock fibres
Abdomen: Pale-yellow seal's fur sub
Rib: Gold thread
Hackle: Pale-yellow cock fibres tied spent

PART 2

The Sedges

Trichoptera

After the *Ephemeroptera* the next most important group of flies of interest to the fisherman are the sedges. Over a period of time most of them have been given accepted common names. Some of these names are descriptive of the insects themselves: Black Sedge, Longhorn Sedge, Cinnamon Sedge, Marbled Sedge, etc. Others are not so obvious – the Welshman's Button, for example.

The sedges are similar to moths but can be distinguished by the lack of a proboscis, which is a long, rolled-up mouth part found on moths just under the front of the head. The other difference is in the wings: moths have tiny scales covering the surface, whereas sedges' wings are covered in hairs. When at rest the sedges' wings are held in a tent shape over the abdomen. Although many species are active towards dusk a few of the species can be seen flying throughout the day.

The following section shows all the sedge flies of interest to the fisherman, along with the type of larvae and case. Cases are open to much local and structural variation so they can only be used as a guide, although the structure is often a good indicator to the species involved. Along with the images of the naturals are suggested artificials; the recipes are given in the text along with the name of the designer where known.

Black Sedge
Silo nigricornis (Plate 47)

The Black Sedge is mostly found in rivers and streams. The larval case is made from coarse sand with a few small stones attached to the sides. It is thought the stones are used to give weight to the case and help prevent it being washed away in the current. This is one of several species that can be parasitized by a small wasp, *Agriotypus*. The wasp crawls under water, finds a suitable caddis and lays a single egg onto the larva. After hatching, the wasp grub feeds on the caddis larva and then pupates in the case. If you find a case with a long filament protruding from the end then the case houses one of these deadly intruders. The adult sedge is seen mostly in the early part of the season and is on the wing from midday onwards. The fly is very dark and stocky.

Larval case:	Sand with small stones attached
Size:	Up to 15mm

Adult:	
Size:	Up to 10mm
Abdomen:	Dark grey
Wings:	Dark grey-black
Habitat:	Mostly rivers and streams
Distribution:	Widespread and common
Time of day:	Midday onwards
Time of year:	May–July

Dressings

1. Black Sedge (Thomas)

DRESSING

Hook length: Up to 10mm
Thread: Black
Abdomen: Black wool
Wing: Black moose hair over abdomen and cut square
Hackle: Black cock

2. Dark Caddis (Jardine)

DRESSING

Hook length: Up to 10mm
Thread: Black
Abdomen: Dark-grey deer hair dubbed
Wing: Brown-black deer hair over abdomen

3. Pebble Caddis Larva (Price)

DRESSING

Hook length: Up to 15mm
Thread: Brown
Case: Green floss covered with vermiculite stuck on with glue
Legs: Brown hen hackle, short
Exposed head/body: Green floss

Watercress
Nasturtium officinale (Plate 47)
Cress family (*Cruciferae*)
Tang-tongue

Flower head:	Clusters of white flowers with yellow anthers held in an erect spike on hollow stems
Leaves:	Rich, green-stalked leaves divided into 5–9 fleshy oval leaflets
Flowering time:	May–October
Height:	Up to 40cm
Habit:	Native perennial
Habitat:	Springs and streams with clean, slow-running water
Distribution:	Common
General:	This common perennial, well-known for its tangy taste, is widespread in the wild but has also been in commercial cultivation since the 1800s when it ▶

133

Plate 47

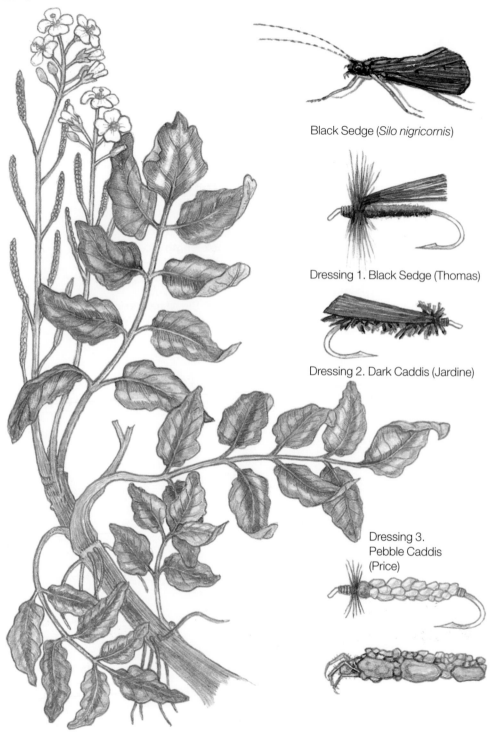

Black Sedge (*Silo nigricornis*)

Dressing 1. Black Sedge (Thomas)

Dressing 2. Dark Caddis (Jardine)

Dressing 3.
Pebble Caddis
(Price)

Watercress (*Nasturtium officinale*)

▶ was first grown in Kent. Often used as a salad ingredient, it is rich in Vitamin C and was eaten in the past in order to prevent scurvy and also to cleanse the blood. *Nasturtium* comes from the Latin *nasi-tortium*, meaning 'nose-twisting', because of the pungent smell the plant gives off

Black Silverhorn
Mystacides azurea (Plate 48)

The silverhorns fall into the family *Leptoceridae* and are recognizable by their long, slim antennae, which may be up to three times the length of the wings. The Black Silverhorn has slim brown-black wings with the main wings disproportionately longer than the rear wings. It can be found in running and still waters, the larvae building shelters out of sand/plant particles. These shelters are long, slender and slightly curved.

Larval case:	Long, slender, curved sand/plant particles
Size:	Up to 15mm

Adult:

Size:	Up to 9mm
Abdomen:	Grey-black
Wings:	Narrow brown-black
Habitat:	Still and running water
Distribution:	Common most areas
Time of day:	Midday onwards
Time of year:	June–August

Dressings
1. Black Sedge (Thomas)

DRESSING

Hook length: Up to 10mm
Thread: Black
Abdomen: Black wool
Wing: Black moose hair full length of hook
Hackle: Black cock

2. Black Silverhorn

DRESSING

Hook length: Up to 10mm
Thread: Black
Abdomen: Magpie herls
Wing: Small black feather tips over abdomen
Hackle: Black cock clipped to a 'V' under
Antennae: Two hackle stalks

3. Caddis Larva (Clarke)

DRESSING

Hook length: Up to 15mm
Thread: Fawn
Case: Pheasant tail fibres, sandy peacock herl
Rib: Copper wire
Legs: Honey hen very short
Exposed head: Fawn wool

Water Figwort
Scrophularia auriculata (Plate 48)
Figwort family (*Scrophulariaceae*)
Water Betony

Flower head:	Numerous dull brownish-red flowers 8–10mm long in loose clusters on square stems

Plate 48

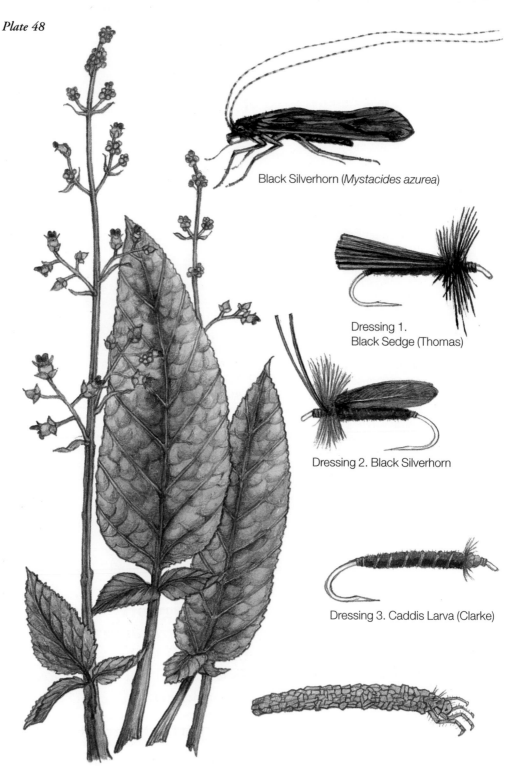

Black Silverhorn (*Mystacides azurea*)

Dressing 1.
Black Sedge (Thomas)

Dressing 2. Black Silverhorn

Dressing 3. Caddis Larva (Clarke)

Water Figwort (*Scrophularia auriculata*)

Leaves:	Opposite pairs of lobed leaves. Each leaf stalk has two small wings at the base		**Larval case:**	Straight, tubular made of sand grains with long twigs attached
Flowering time:	June–September		**Size:**	Up to 40mm
Height:	Up to 120cm			
Habit:	Perennial		**Adult:**	
Habitat:	Wet places, ponds, streamsides, damp woods		**Size:**	Up to 15mm
			Abdomen:	Brown
Distribution:	Common in England. especially the south; rare in Wales, Scotland and Ireland		**Wings:**	Dark reddish-brown
			Habitat:	Still and running water
			Distribution:	Common
			Time of day:	Mid-afternoon onwards
General:	Water Figwort, which is a common sight alongside areas of water and in wet places, is a rather dull, undistinguished-looking plant. In the past its leaves were gathered and crushed to help make an ointment which was used to soothe swellings		**Time of year**:	June–October, peak around September

Brown Sedge
Anabolia nervosa (Plate 49)

Anabolia is found in both rivers and lakes, the larva building a rather unusual case. The central tube is made from coarse sand grains to which are attached longer twigs; it is said that the case is so designed to deter fish and birds from eating it. The larva's head is fawny-yellow with distinct black markings; its movement is fairly cumbersome because of the case design. The adult sedge is often seen in large swarms on late summer and early autumn evenings. It is of medium size with fairly broad wings. The antennae are roughly the same length as the wings.

Dressings

1. Brown Sedge (Price)

DRESSING

Hook length: Up to 15mm
Thread: Orange
Abdomen: Cinnamon turkey fibres twisted in with gold wire
Wing: Two brown-red hackle tips length of abdomen
Hackle: Very short red game palmered down abdomen, a normal size hackle at head

2. Brown Sedge (Conba)

DRESSING

Hook length: Up to 15mm
Thread: Black
Abdomen: Golden pheasant herls
Rib: Gold wire
Wing: Golden pheasant herls over abdomen
Hackle: Red-brown cock palmered length of body, head hackle red-brown cock normal length

Plate 49

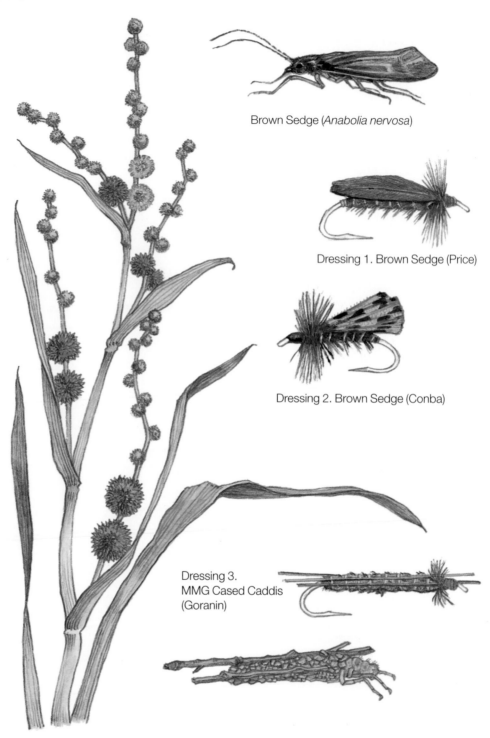

Brown Sedge (*Anabolia nervosa*)

Dressing 1. Brown Sedge (Price)

Dressing 2. Brown Sedge (Conba)

Dressing 3.
MMG Cased Caddis
(Goranin)

Branched Bur Reed (*Sparganium erectum*)

3. MMG Cased Caddis (Goranin)

DRESSING

Hook length: Up to 20mm
Thread: Brown
Abdomen: A mix of brown hackle fibres, grizzle hackle fibres and brown seal's fur all mixed and dubbed. Any long fibres are cut off except at the head
Rib: Gold wire
Sticks: Three hackle stalks tied in at the eye and bent and left longer than hook
Legs: See abdomen

Branched Bur Reed
Sparganium erectum (Plate 49)
Bur Reed family (*Sparganiaceae*)

Flower head:	Tiny, globe-like flower heads carried at the top of erect, zigzag stems that are branched in the upper part. Each head is made of either male or female flowers only – male flowers at the top of stems, female flowers lower down. Female flower heads are larger than male ones and fewer in number
Leaves:	Grass-like leaves are stiff and erect. They are triangular near the base, have parallel veining and a distinct keel on the underside. Bases of the leaves form sheaths round the stems and occasionally float on the surface
Flowering time:	June–August
Height:	Up to 1.5m
Habit:	Perennial
Habitat:	Shallow water, ponds, ditches

Distribution:	Common except in northern Scotland
General:	This hairless perennial, which is the most common of the bur reeds, is often found growing in large clumps in stagnant or slow-flowing water rich in nutrients. Its name is taken from the prickly bur-like fruit produced by the female flowers

Brown Silverhorn
Athripsodes albifrons, cinereus (Plate 50)

Brown Silverhorns can be found in fairly large swarms on summer evenings, usually under overhanging branches of trees. They generally appear from midday onwards and fly low over the surface of the water, where, occasionally, casualties fall prey to the waiting trout. The larvae make their case from sand/plant particles. *Athripsodes albifrons* in the adult stage is brown with white bars on the wings; *cinereus* is a similar colour but without the markings. Both species have the long, slim antennae typical of the family *Leptoceridae*.

Larval case:	Long, slender, sand/plant particles, slightly curved
Size:	Up to 18mm
Adult:	
Size:	Up to 10mm
Abdomen:	Dark greyish-brown
Wings:	Brown, or brown with white bars
Habitat:	Still waters and rivers
Distribution:	Common and widespread
Time of day:	Midday onwards
Time of year:	Warm summer months, mid-June–August

Plate 50

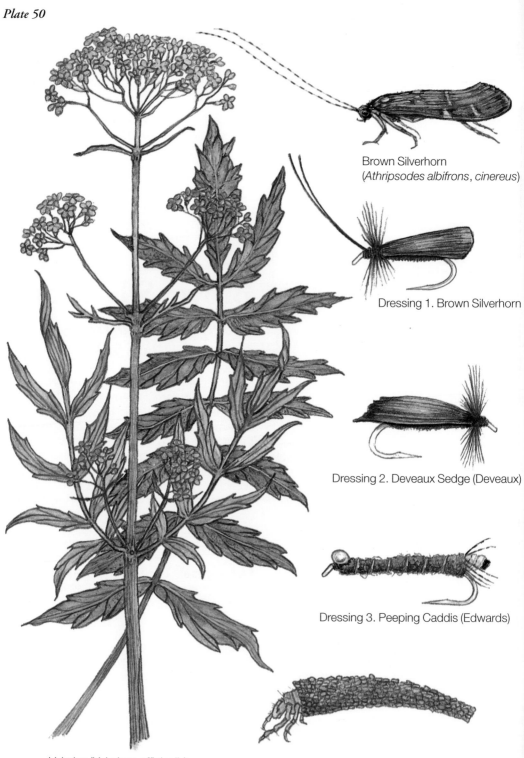

Brown Silverhorn
(*Athripsodes albifrons*, *cinereus*)

Dressing 1. Brown Silverhorn

Dressing 2. Deveaux Sedge (Deveaux)

Dressing 3. Peeping Caddis (Edwards)

Valerian (*Valeriana officinalis*)

Dressings

1. Brown Silverhorn

DRESSING

Hook length: Up to 10mm
Thread: Brown
Abdomen: A mix of grey and brown seal's fur dubbing
Wing: Dark grey-brown feather fibres slightly longer than hook and trimmed to shape
Hackle: Dull-brown cock
Antennae: Two hackle stalks

2. Deveaux Sedge (Deveaux)

DRESSING

Hook length: Up to 10mm
Thread: Brown
Abdomen: Dark grey-brown dubbing
Wing: Brown mallard in tent shape over and slightly longer than abdomen
Hackle: Dull-brown cock

3. Peeping Caddis (Edwards)

DRESSING

Hook length: Up to 15mm
Thread: Brown
Case: Hare's fur
Rib: Gold wire
Legs: Short partridge hackle
Exposed head: Pale fawny-coloured wool burnt at tip to make a black head at the bend end. At the eye end of the hook a lead shot is added to provide weight

Valerian
Valeriana officinalis (Plate 50)
Valerian family (*Valerianaceae*)

Flower head:	Clusters of small flesh- to pale-pink florets carried together on short stalks at the top of the stems
Leaves:	Dark-green upper surface, lighter underneath with margins toothed at intervals. Lower leaves are long-stalked, the upper ones stalkless and carried in pairs up the stem. Each leaf is divided into 4–8 pairs of leaflets
Flowering time:	July–September
Height:	Up to 1.2m
Habit:	Native perennial
Habitat:	Rough, damp grass, damp places on banks of streams and rivers
Distribution:	Common
General:	This hairy, robust perennial has been used since the middle ages in the treatment of various ailments. Valerian comes from the Latin valere, meaning 'to heal'. When crushed, the plant gives off a very pungent smell – the dried root was put amongst clean linen to scent it. In the First World War Valerian was used for calming people suffering from shock, and in many countries is still drunk in the form of a tea as an antidote to nervous disorders

Caperer
Halesus radiatus, digitatus (Plate 51)

The Caperer is one of the largest of the sedges and can be found on both rivers and still waters. It is a fly mostly found later in the season from the end of August onwards, and hatches usually occur from late afternoon well into the evening. It is easily confused with the Large Cinnamon Sedge, being very similar in size and colour. From a fishing point of view this is of little importance as the same artificial flies will do for both species. The larva builds a case very similar to *Anabolia*, the Brown Sedge, but the central tube is made almost entirely of vegetable matter.

Larval case:	Plant material with sticks attached
Size:	Up to 27mm
Adult:	
Size:	Up to 23mm
Abdomen:	Orange-brown
Wings:	Pale orange-brown with darker markings
Habitat:	Still waters and rivers
Distribution:	Fairly common and widespread
Time of day:	Late afternoon onwards
Time of year:	August–October

Dressings

1. Caperer (Lunn)

DRESSING

Hook length: Up to 15mm
Thread: Crimson
Abdomen: Turkey herls from the tail feather front and rear with a centre section of swan herls dyed yellow
Wing: Yellow-brown feather
Hackle: Black and red cock wound in together

2. Emergent Caddis (LaFontaine)

DRESSING

Hook length: Up to 15mm
Thread: Orange
Abdomen: Sparkle yarn and fur mixed orange, cream and brown. Over this a loose covering of clear brown and orange sparkle yarn tied in at head and tail of hook
Wing: Orange-brown deer hair
Head: Orange-brown marabou fibres

3. Green Twig Caddis

DRESSING

Hook length: Up to 20mm
Thread: Brown
Case: Dull-green dubbing or floss, a few feather stalks attached
Exposed body: Yellow floss
Legs: Very short brown hackle

Fleabane
Pulicaria dysenterica (Plate 51)
Daisy family (*Compositae*)

Flower head:	Yellow daisy-like flowers up to 3cm in diameter and carried in loose, flat-topped clusters. Central ring of deeper-yellow tubular florets surrounded by a ring of golden-yellow ray florets
Leaves:	Alternate with soft, wavy edges, the lower surface densely covered with downy hairs. Lower leaves are oval and narrow into a stalk, upper leaves are ▶

Plate 51

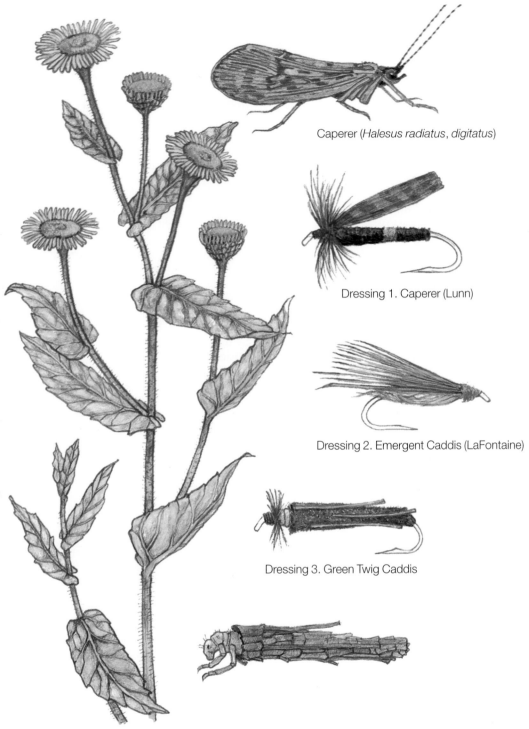

Caperer (*Halesus radiatus*, *digitatus*)

Dressing 1. Caperer (Lunn)

Dressing 2. Emergent Caddis (LaFontaine)

Dressing 3. Green Twig Caddis

Fleabane (*Pulicaria dysenterica*)

▶ more heart-shaped with the base clasping the stem

Flowering time: July–September
Height: Up to 60 cm
Habit: Native perennial
Habitat: Marshes, wet meadows, ditches, hedgerows and ponds
Distribution: Common, except Scotland and northern England
General: This is one of several plants which were given the common name of fleabane. All of them when dried were placed in beds or scattered amongst the grasses strewn on floors in olden times. The leaves when crushed give off a soapy smell which fleas find very attractive, yet the juices destroy them. Fleabane is also attractive to other insects and several butterflies use it as a foodplant. *Pulicaria* comes from the Latin *pulex* – 'flea' – whilst *dysenterica* possibly refers to it being a cause or a cure for dysentery

Cinnamon Sedge
Limnephilus lunatus
(Plate 52)

The Cinnamon Sedge is a fly of still waters and rivers. With its cinnamon-brown wings and distinctive mottled markings it is easily identified. The rear of the main wings is clearly marked with a crescent 'lunar' shadow effect. It is another fairly common species, found from June well into the autumn. The larva builds a case from a variety of materials which can include plant materials and shells.

Larval case: Cylindrical case made from various materials including plant and shells
Size: Up to 23mm

Adult:
Size: Up to 15mm
Abdomen: Green
Wings: Cinnamon with contrasting markings and crescent
Location: Still and running water
Distribution: Common, widespread
Time of day: Midday onwards
Time of year: June–October

Dressings

1. Balloon Sedge

DRESSING

Hook length: Up to 15mm
Thread: Orange
Abdomen: Green-brown poly dubbing
Wing: Orange-brown deer hair
Head: Mustard-coloured fly foam or polycelon

Plate 52

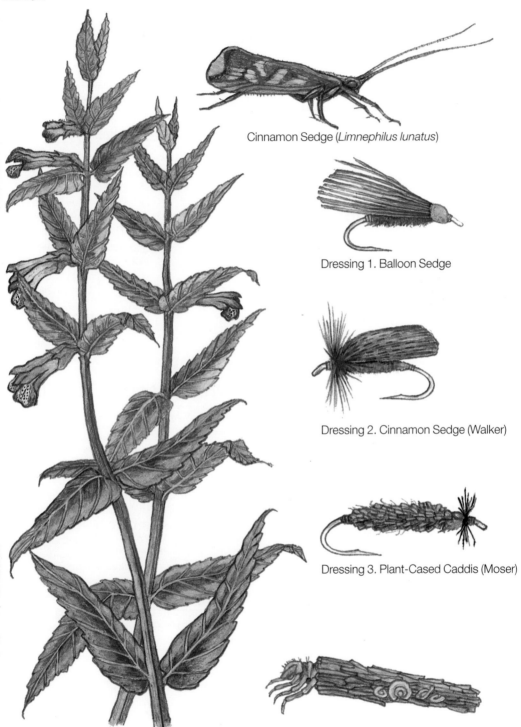

Cinnamon Sedge (*Limnephilus lunatus*)

Dressing 1. Balloon Sedge

Dressing 2. Cinnamon Sedge (Walker)

Dressing 3. Plant-Cased Caddis (Moser)

Skullcap (*Scutellaria galericulata*)

2. Cinnamon Sedge (Walker)

DRESSING

Hook length: Up to 15mm
Thread: Orange
Abdomen: Buff ostrich herls with a tag of fluorescent yellow floss
Wing: Barred cinnamon cock fibres
Hackle: Ginger cock

3. Plant-Cased Caddis (Moser)

DRESSING

Hook length: Up to 20mm
Thread: Brown
Case: Brown and green dubbing with clipped deer hair mixed in
Exposed body: Yellow hare's ear with a thin piece of brown Latex over
Legs: Black cock hackle short

Skullcap
Scutellaria galericulata
(Plate 52)
Mint family (*Labiatae*)
(Helmet flower)

Flower head:	10–12mm long, bluish-violet in colour with the lower lip usually lighter. Flowers are in groups of 1–4 lower down the plant and carried singly higher up; all arise from the leaf axils
Leaves:	Short-stalked with shallowly toothed margins and carried in opposite pairs
Flowering time:	June–September
Height:	Up to 50cm

Habit:	Perennial
Habitat:	Wet meadows, damp, sheltered places at watersides
Distribution:	Common except Ireland and Scotland
General:	This creeping perennial can often be found in large patches at the waterside. Its common names of skullcap or helmet flower refer to the shape of the calyx, which resembles a small helmet. The plant has been used in the treatment of malaria and also contains scutellarin oil, which is very useful in treating nervous disorders and hysteria

Grannom
Brachycentrus subnubilus
(Plate 53)

The Grannom is an early season sedge and is found from early April into June. It is a fly of medium, fast-flowing water and can be found on both chalk streams and stony rivers. It is fairly widespread but can be localized in its distribution. Where it does occur in sufficient numbers it can be of great interest to the fly fisherman, bringing on an early rise of fish at the start of the season. Some artificial patterns have a distinctive green tag at the rear of the abdomen; this is to represent the mass of green eggs that the female carries and releases into the water. The egg ball can number up to 700 eggs. The larval case is made from a chitin-like material which is sometimes anchored to stones or vegetation. It can be cylindrical or almost square, sectioned with a slight taper.

Larval case:	Made from a chitin-like material
Size:	Up to 20mm

Plate 53

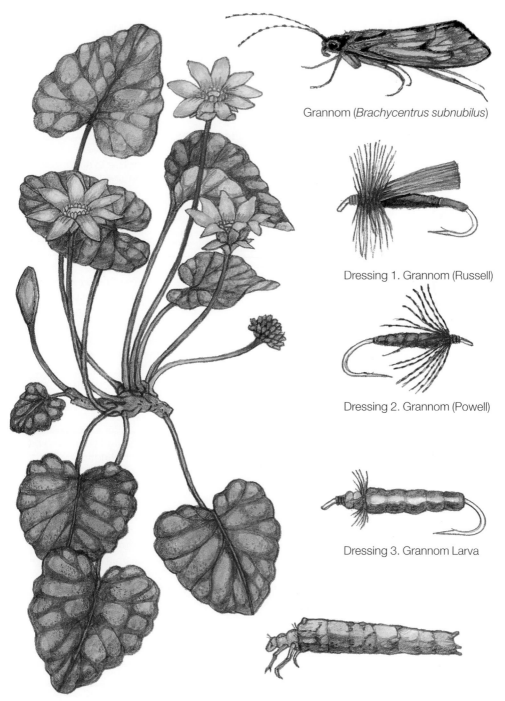

Grannom (*Brachycentrus subnubilus*)

Dressing 1. Grannom (Russell)

Dressing 2. Grannom (Powell)

Dressing 3. Grannom Larva

Lesser Celandine (*Ranunculus ficaria*)

Adult:
Size: Up to 12mm
Abdomen: Dark olive-green
Wings: Grey-brown to pale orange-brown with darker markings
Habitat: Weedy and stony rivers with a fair flow
Distribution: Widespread, can be localized
Time of day: Midday onwards
Time of year: April–June

Dressings

1. Grannom (Russell)

DRESSING
Hook length: Up to 12mm **Thread**: Green **Abdomen**: A tip of green wool or similar, rest of body heron herl **Wing**: Blue-dun hackle fibres cut to length **Hackle**: Brown-ginger cock

2. Grannom (Powell)

DRESSING
Hook length: Up to 12mm **Thread**: Green **Abdomen**: Olive-coloured mole fur **Hackle**: Grey partridge

3. Grannom Larva

DRESSING
Hook length: Up to 20mm **Thread**: Brown **Case**: Brown floss covered with overlapping turns of pale brown-grey polythene strip **Exposed body**: Green floss **Legs**: Short brown hackle

Lesser Celandine
Ranunculus ficaria (**Plate 53**)
Buttercup family (*Ranunculaceae*)
(Pilewort)

Flower head: Shiny yellow individual flowers with 8–12 glossy petals in a star-shaped flower. Each flower is carried at the end of a long stalk and is about 2.5cm in diameter
Leaves: Heart to kidney-shaped leaves at the end of long stalks and forming a loose rosette. Dark green in colour and with a glossy appearance, often with darker or lighter shading
Flowering time: March–May
Height: Up to 15cm
Habit: Native perennial
Habitat: Meadows, riverbanks, damp woodland
Distribution: Common
General: Lesser Celandine is one of the first flowers to be seen in springtime with its flowers opening wide in bright sunshine and closing in duller weather. It is one of the *Ranunculus* or buttercup family, *Ranunculus* being taken from the Latin *rana* – 'frog' – a reference to the damp places in which the plant is found. One of its common names is pilewort as Lesser Celandine is used in a traditional cure for this disorder. Occasionally the plant's leaves were boiled and eaten as a vegetable

Great Red Sedge

Phryganea grandis, striata (Plate 54)

This is the largest species of sedge fly in Britain and can attain a length of up to 25mm in the adult stage. It is a fly of still waters and slower flowing rivers; in Ireland it is found on the larger lakes and referred to as the Murragh. It is said that the larva will devour small fish and with its 40mm length this is quite believable. The larva's case is made from plant material arranged in a spiral shape and can be up to 50mm long by 9mm wide. Although there are several species of *Phryganea*, the two of interest to the fisherman are *grandis* and *striata*. Wings can vary from brown-red to a pale grey-brown with darker markings.

Larval case:	Made from plant fragments in a spiral pattern
Size:	Very large, up to 50mm
Adult:	
Size:	Up to 25mm
Abdomen:	Grey to grey-green
Wings:	Pale grey-brown to red-brown with darker markings
Habitat:	Still waters and slower-flowing rivers
Distribution:	Widespread
Time of day:	Late afternoon onwards
Time of year:	Odd specimens from mid-May into August but mostly June–July

Dressings

1. Great Red Sedge (Collyer)

DRESSING

Hook length: Up to 22mm
Thread: Brown
Tail: Red cock fibres
Abdomen: Grey mole, a dark-red cock palmered length of body
Rib: Gold wire
Wing: Speckled feather tied in length of abdomen and sloping
Hackle: Dark-red cock

2. Sedge (Ruane)

DRESSING

Hook length: Up to 22mm
Thread: Green
Abdomen: Green poly dub
Wings: Cut out of Fly-Rite, pale brown
Antennae: Two paintbrush bristles
Legs: Deer hair dyed green

3. Cased Caddis (Carnill)

DRESSING

Hook length: Up to 26mm
Thread: Black
Abdomen: Grey-brown-olive fur
Exposed body: Cream herl
Legs: Short black hen hackle
Exposed head: Fawn wool

Plate 54

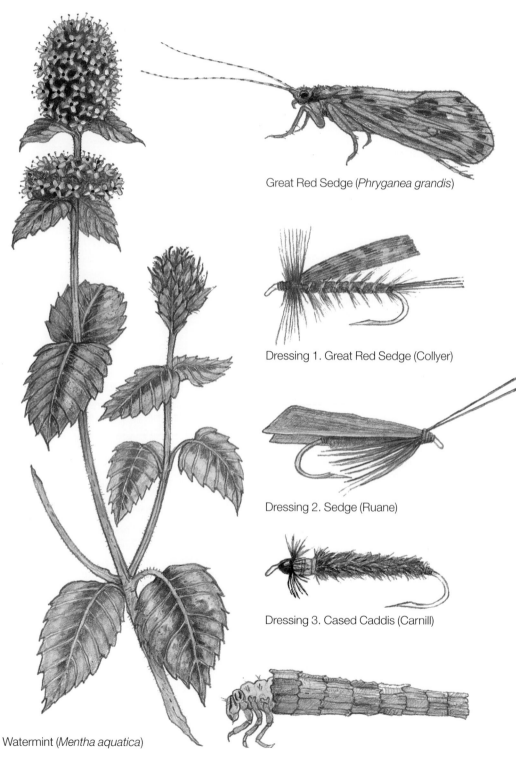

Great Red Sedge (*Phryganea grandis*)

Dressing 1. Great Red Sedge (Collyer)

Dressing 2. Sedge (Ruane)

Dressing 3. Cased Caddis (Carnill)

Watermint (*Mentha aquatica*)

Watermint
Mentha aquatica (**Plate 54**)
Mint family (*Labiatae*)

Flower head:	Dense rounded whorls of pink or whitish flowers at the end of the stems or in the upper axils
Leaves:	Opposite pairs of hairy, bluntly toothed leaves, each at 90 degrees to the next pair
Flowering time:	July–October
Height:	Up to 90cm
Habit:	Native perennial
Habitat:	River and stream banks, damp places, in water
Distribution:	Common except for the far north
General:	This is the commonest and most widespread of all the mint family. It can be difficult to identify as when present with other species of mint it will readily hybridize. When crushed, both leaves and flowers give off a highly aromatic scent

Grey Flag
Hydropsyche instabilis (**Plate 55**)

The *Hydropsyche* species are unusual in that they will fly in bright sunshine, and so can be of special interest to the fisherman. The larvae are of the free-swimming type, building only flimsy nets in which to trap their food. They are mostly found in fast-running rivers and streams. The Grey Flag is a fairly inconspicuous fly with dull grey wings with some contrasting markings. Although widespread it is not found in great numbers.

Larval case:	None
Size:	Up to 18mm
Adult:	
Size:	Up to 14mm
Abdomen:	Grey-brown
Wings:	Grey-brown with some contrasting markings
Habitat:	Fast-flowing streams and rivers
Distribution:	Widespread
Time of day:	Anytime of day even in bright sunlight
Time of year:	Mid-June–September

Dressings

1. Grey Sedge (Veniard)

DRESSING

Hook length: Up to 12mm
Thread: Grey
Abdomen: Grey seal's fur sub
Rib: Silver wire
Wing: Fibres from tail of grey squirrel
Hackle: Grizzle cock

Plate 55

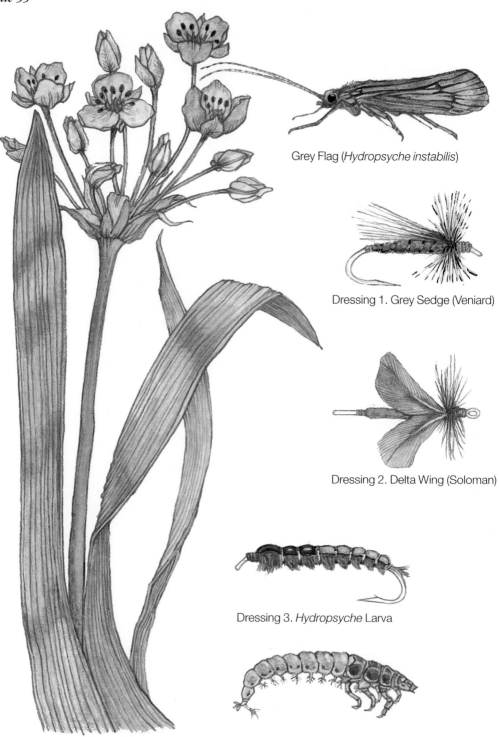

Grey Flag (*Hydropsyche instabilis*)

Dressing 1. Grey Sedge (Veniard)

Dressing 2. Delta Wing (Soloman)

Dressing 3. *Hydropsyche* Larva

Flowering Rush (*Butomus umbellatus*)

3. *Hydropsyche* Larva

DRESSING

Hook length: Up to 18mm
Thread: Brown
Abdomen: Hare's fur well picked out of thorax area and for tail
Back: Clear Latex with first three segments coloured dark brown
Rib: Silver wire

2. Delta Wing Sedge (Soloman)

DRESSING

Hook length: Up to 12mm
Thread: Grey
Abdomen: Pale mink fur
Wings: Grey feather tips tied in a 'V' shape
Hackle: Brown cock trimmed under

Flowering Rush
Butomus umbellatus (Plate 55)
Flowering Rush family
(*Butomaceae*)
(Grassy Rush, Water Gladiolus)

Flower head:	An umbrella-shaped flower head up to 2.5cm in diameter, made up of 10–30 flowers. Flowers are pink in colour with a deeper pink veining, long-stalked and made up of 3 petals and 3 smaller outer sepals
Leaves:	Leaves are all basal and as tall as the stem, triangular in cross-section, and all stiffly erect, dark green to greyish-green in colour
Flowering time:	July–August
Height:	Up to 1.5m
Habit:	Native perennial
Habitat:	Ponds, ditches, canals and river edges, slow-moving waters
Distribution:	Localized throughout Britain except in Scotland
General:	This is an attractive-looking plant often used as an ornamental species in gardens. When growing in the wild it has a preference for waterways where the bottom is made up of thick, rich mud. The leaves have very sharp edges and are avoided by cattle but were once harvested and used in basket weaving and mat making. In parts of Russia the fleshy rootstock is collected and eaten as a source of food, sometimes powdered for bread

Grouse Wing Sedge
Mystacides longicornis (Plate 56)

This sedge has fairly long and narrow wings with distinctive barred markings similar to a grouse feather. It inhabits still waters and can be found almost anywhere in the British Isles. It is a fly of the late afternoon and evenings. The Grouse Wing has long antennae at least twice the length of the body. The larvae build slightly curved cases made from sand grains with twigs or other vegetable material.

Larval case:	Slender, slightly curved, made from sand and vegetation
Size:	Up to 14mm

153

Plate 56

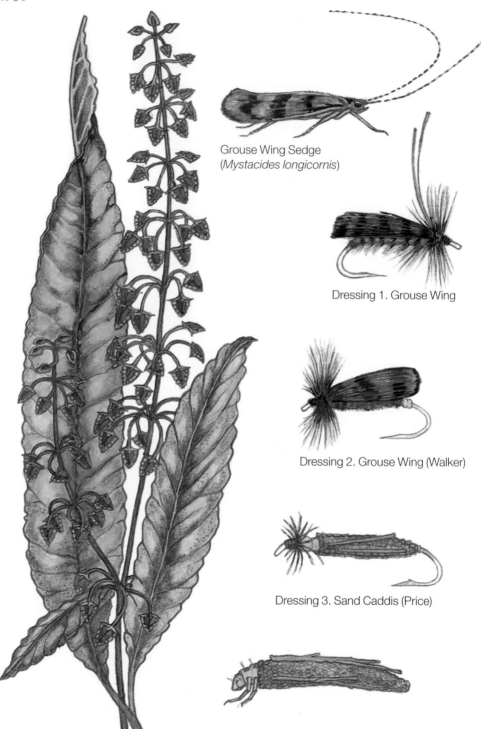

Grouse Wing Sedge
(*Mystacides longicornis*)

Dressing 1. Grouse Wing

Dressing 2. Grouse Wing (Walker)

Dressing 3. Sand Caddis (Price)

Great Water Dock (*Purnex hydrolaparthum*)

Adult:
Size:	Up to 9mm
Abdomen:	Dark brown
Wings:	Grey-yellow with three brown stripes
Habitat:	Still waters, very rare on rivers
Distribution:	Common and widespread
Time of day:	After midday
Time of year:	Late May–September

Dressings

1. Grouse Wing)

DRESSING

Hook length: Up to 9mm
Thread: Brown
Abdomen: Dark hare's fur
Wing: Well-marked partridge
Hackle: Dull-brown cock full at head and palmered length of abdomen
Antennae: Hackle stalks

2. Grouse Wing (Walker)

DRESSING

Hook length: Up to 10mm
Thread: Black
Abdomen: Dark-brown ostrich herl with a tag of white floss
Wing: Grouse feather or similar
Hackle: Furnace cock

3. Sand Caddis (Price)

DRESSING

Hook length: Up to 15mm
Thread: Brown
Abdomen: Floss coated in cement then fine sand; hackle stalks can be added if desired
Exposed body: Cream floss
Legs: Brown hen hackle, short

Great Water Dock
Rumex hydrolaparthum
(Plate 56)
Dock family (*Polygonaceae*)

Flower head:	Individual, inconspicuous flowers carried above the leaves in loose spikes
Leaves:	Lance-shaped leaves, the lower ones up to 80cm long
Flowering time:	July–September
Height:	Up to 2m
Habit:	Perennial
Habitat:	Shallow water, reedbeds, stagnant, slow-flowing water
Distribution:	Fairly common and widespread
General:	This familiar-looking member of the dock family is found not only by watersides but also on waste ground that may become temporarily flooded. It is a close relative of the more common dock, the leaves of which children rub on nettle stings to take away the tingling sensation. An infusion of its roots is used in herbal medicine as a mouthwash

155

Large Cinnamon Sedge
Potamophylax latipennis
(Plate 57)

This fly is very similar in shape and colour to *Halesus radiatus*, the Caperer, and the same patterns can be used for either. Although mainly a river fly, it is also found on still waters. Along with some of the other sandy-coloured sedges it seems particularly appealing to feeding trout. The larva builds a case of sand or gravel, the colour depending on the natural building materials available. It is the kind of case that is fairly easy to copy and also a larva which fish are fond of taking. The natural is slow-moving and the artificial should be left to drift slowly along the riverbed.

Larval case:	Fine sand and gravel, slight curve
Size:	Up to 25mm
Adult:	
Size:	18–20mm
Abdomen:	Colour can vary between sandy-brown and green-brown
Wings:	Sandy-brown with darker markings
Habitat:	Still and flowing water
Distribution:	Widespread and common
Time of day:	Evenings
Time of year:	June–September

Dressings

1. G & H Sedge (Goddard and Henry)

> **DRESSING**
>
> **Hook length**: Up to 20mm
> **Thread**: Green
> **Abdomen**: Green fur
> **Wing**: Deer hair colour to natural
> **Hackle**: Rusty-dun cock
> **Antennae**: The hackle stalks from the hackle feather

2. Caddis Larva (Bradbury)

> **DRESSING**
>
> **Hook length**: Up to 20mm
> **Thread**: Brown
> **Case**: Mottled feather fibres and fur
> **Rib**: Gold wire
> **Legs**: Brown partridge
> **Exposed head**: Peacock herl

3. Rubbery Caddis (O'Reilly)

> **DRESSING**
>
> **Hook length**: Up to 20mm
> **Thread**: Brown
> **Case**: An elastic band is wound on the hook and covered in glue; grit is then sprinkled onto the still-wet glue
> **Legs**: Brown hackle
> **Exposed head**: Brown thread

Plate 57

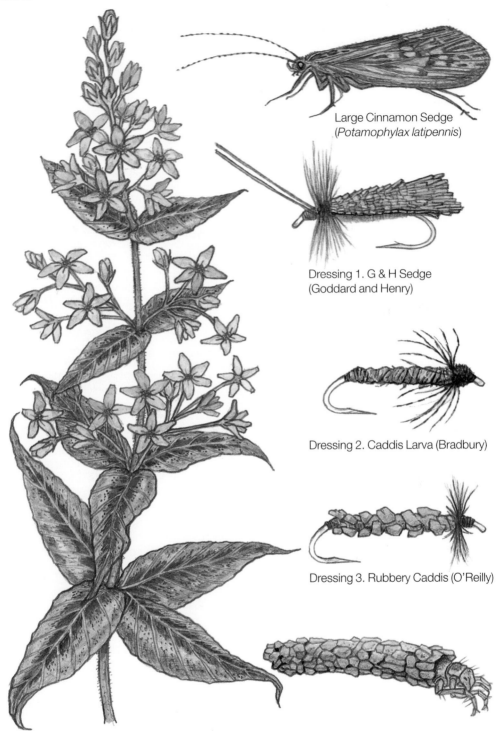

Large Cinnamon Sedge
(*Potamophylax latipennis*)

Dressing 1. G & H Sedge
(Goddard and Henry)

Dressing 2. Caddis Larva (Bradbury)

Dressing 3. Rubbery Caddis (O'Reilly)

Yellow Loosestrife (*Lysimachia vulgaris*)

Yellow Loosestrife
Lysimachia vulgaris (Plate 57)
Primrose family (*Primulaceae*)
(Yellow Willowherb)

Flower head:	Cup-shaped yellow flowers 1–2cm across and forming loose clusters at the top of the stems. The flowers, which are scentless and contain no pollen, are made up of five petals and five sepals, the latter having orange margins. Stems are slightly angular, brown or green in colour and hairy
Leaves:	Oval or spear-shaped and up to 12cm long, the leaves are bright green above and bluish-green on their undersides. The upper surfaces are dotted with orange or black glands. Leaves occur either in opposite pairs or whorls of 3–4 and are almost stalkless
Fruit:	Round capsules approximately 5mm in diameter
Flowering time:	July–August
Height:	Up to 1m
Habit:	Perennial
Habitat:	Rivers and lakesides, fens, marshes and wet meadows
Distribution:	Fairly common and widespread, except for Scotland
General:	This is a native perennial with far-reaching rhizomes, often found growing in clumps. According to legend it was named after King Lysimachus, an ancient king of Thrace who discovered the plant's medicinal properties. An alternative version of the origin of the plant's name is that when bunches of the flowers were tied to the necks of draft animals it would prevent them becoming agitated when working together, *Lysimachia* coming from the Greek *lysis* – 'releasing' – and *mache*, 'strife'. According to the herbalist Culpepper, Loosestrife was useful in treating all kinds of bleeding and as a gargle for sore mouths. Smoke from it was also useful for driving away flies and gnats, which proved a nuisance to people living near marsh and fen country

Plate 58

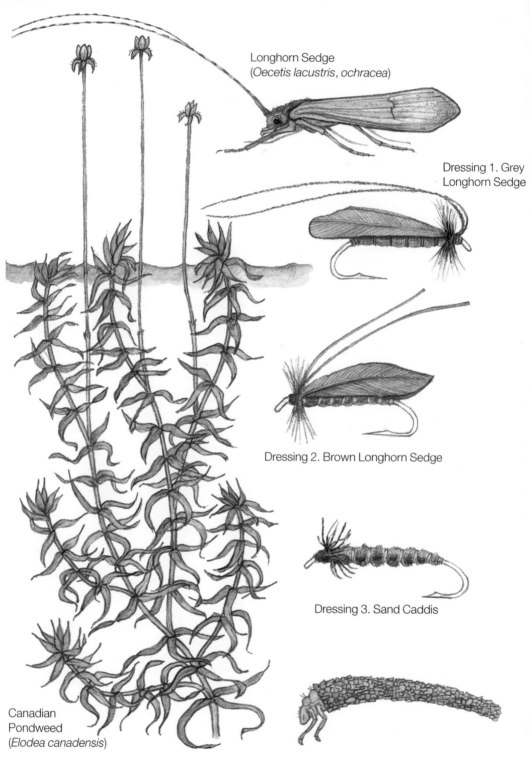

Longhorn Sedge
(*Oecetis lacustris, ochracea*)

Dressing 1. Grey
Longhorn Sedge

Dressing 2. Brown Longhorn Sedge

Dressing 3. Sand Caddis

Canadian
Pondweed
(*Elodea canadensis*)

Flowering time: May–October
Height: Up to 3m
Habit: Introduced perennial
Habitat: Slow-moving waters
Distribution: Widespread
General: Introduced from Canada in the nineteenth century, this plant rapidly spread and often gave problems with blocked waterways. In some countries it is referred to as 'water plague' and in Worcestershire was known as 'drain devil'. The leafy stems remain totally submerged by water with only the tiny flower appearing at the surface. The plant produces large amounts of oxygen and so is widely grown in aquaria

Marbled Sedge

Hydropsyche contubernalis (Plate 59)

This is a fairly distinctive sedge with pale grey-brown wings with darker blotches and patches. Mostly found on rivers and streams it is occasionally found on still waters with some form of flow. It is said to have a preference for shady areas, particularly around heavy vegetation. The larva is yellowish to brownish-grey and builds irregular-shaped nets to catch food. The front three segments and the head are darker than the rest of the body. The underside of the body carries the gill filaments.

Larval case: None, free-swimming
Size: Up to 18mm

Adult:
Size: Up to 12mm
Abdomen: Green

Wings: Marbled pale grey with darker markings
Habitat: Mostly rivers and streams
Distribution: Widespread
Time of day: After midday
Time of year: June–September, mostly July–August

Dressings

1. Marbled Sedge

> **DRESSING**
>
> **Hook length**: Up to 12mm
> **Thread**: Brown
> **Abdomen**: Dark-green seal's fur sub
> **Wing**: Very pale, well-marked hen pheasant
> **Hackle**: Grizzle, well marked

2. Latex Cream Caddis (Price)

> **DRESSING**
>
> **Hook length**: Up to 18mm, curved
> **Thread**: Brown
> **Abdomen**: Pale-brown ostrich herl
> **Rib**: Creamy-yellow Latex (this is a wide rib leaving only narrow bands of herl showing)
> **Thorax area**: Dark-brown seal's fur sub
> **Legs**: Brown partridge

3. Caseless Caddis (Klinken)

> **DRESSING**
>
> **Hook length**: Up to 18mm
> **Thread**: Black
> **Abdomen**: Creamy-coloured furry foam or similar
> **Back**: Yellow flexibody front sections coloured with black waterproof marker pen
> **Rib**: Clear, strong mono
> **Thorax**: Mink body fur well picked out

Plate 59

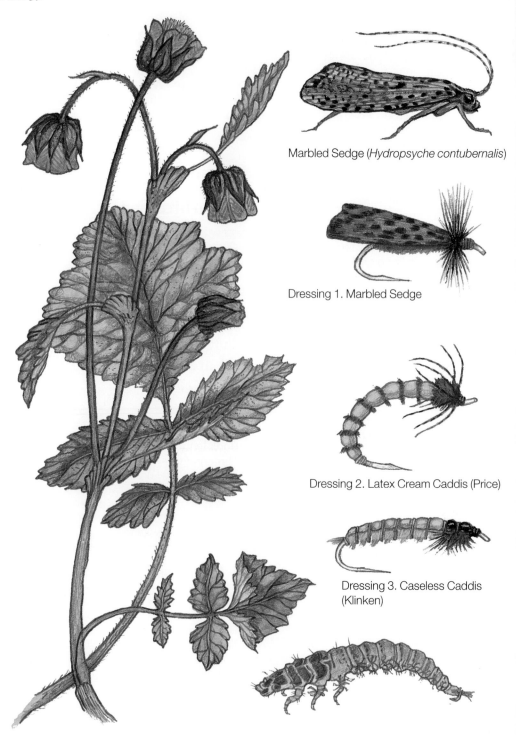

Marbled Sedge (*Hydropsyche contubernalis*)

Dressing 1. Marbled Sedge

Dressing 2. Latex Cream Caddis (Price)

Dressing 3. Caseless Caddis (Klinken)

Water Avens (*Geum rivale*)

Water Avens
Geum rivale (Plate 59)
Rose family (*Rosaceae*)
(Indian Chocolate, Purple Avens)

Flower head:	Drooping, bell-shaped flowers with dullish orange-pink petals and deep reddish-brown sepals carried singly on slender stalks
Leaves:	Opposite pairs of toothed leaflets, the end leaflet being the largest
Flowering time:	April–September
Height:	Up to 60cm
Habit:	Native perennial
Habitat:	Wet meadows, woodland, damp, shady places and streamsides
Distribution:	Common except southern England and northern Scotland
General:	This slightly hairy perennial with nodding bell-shaped flower heads is more common in the wetter northern areas of Britain. If present with other members of the family it may be found in a hybridized form which has characteristics of both parent plants. Distribution of the plant is ensured by the presence of tiny burs on the seed heads, which attach themselves to fur or clothing and so are carried away from the parent plant

Medium Sedge
Goera pilosa (Plate 60)

This is a fairly common, drab-looking sedge, usually greyish-yellow in colour with reasonably short antennae. It is found on rivers and streams with a fairly fast flow. The larva builds a straight-sided tube from sand grains with larger stones attached to the sides, thought to act as a form of ballast to prevent the structure being washed downstream. This is another species of sedge like *Silo nigricornis*, the Black Sedge, that is preyed upon by the small wasp *Agriolypus* (see under Black Sedge).

Larval case:	Made up of sand with a few larger stones down each side
Size:	Up to 16mm
Adult:	
Size:	Up to 12mm
Abdomen:	Pale greyish-yellow
Wings:	Greyish-yellow
Habitat:	Rivers and streams
Distribution:	Well distributed and fairly abundant
Time of day:	Throughout the day
Time of year:	May–July

Dressings

1. Medium Sedge

DRESSING
Hook length: Up to 12mm
Thread: Yellow
Abdomen: Mixed grey and yellow seal's fur sub
Rib: Gold thread
Wing: Very pale hen pheasant
Hackle: Palest ginger trimmed to a 'V' under

Plate 60

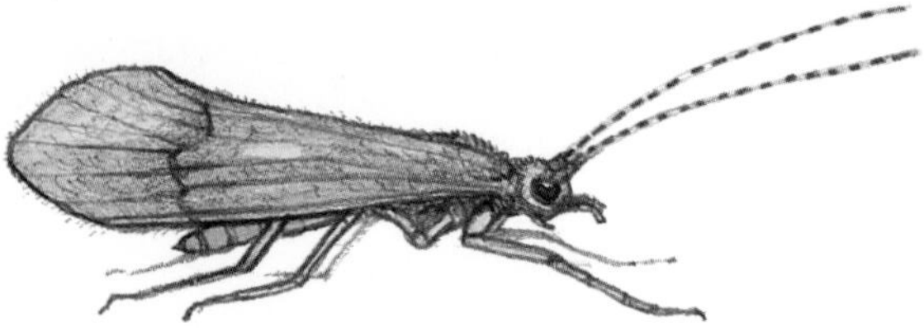

Medium Sedge (*Goera pilosa*)

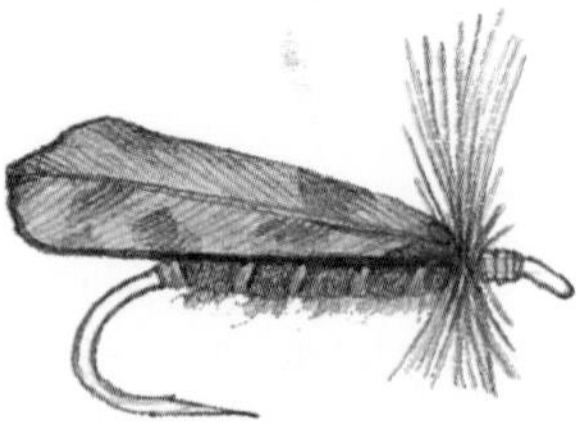

Dressing 1. Medium Sedge

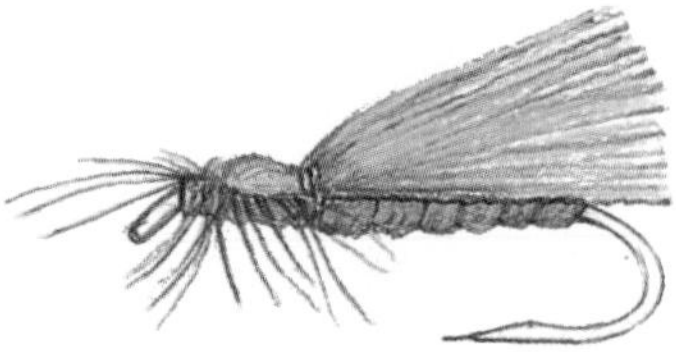

Dressing 2. Para-Poly Sedge (Klinken)

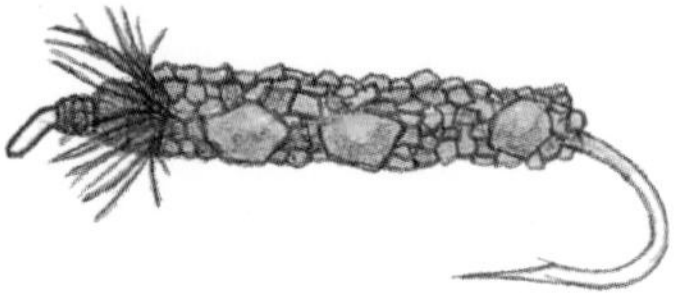

Dressing 3. Pebble Caddis (Price)

Gipsywort (*Lycopus europaeus*)

2. Para-Poly Sedge (Klinken)

DRESSING

Hook length: Up to 12mm
Thread: Pale yellow
Abdomen: Pale grey-yellow Fly-Rite poly dubbing
Wing: Poly yarn, yellow-grey, tied at head and a little way back to give a wing shape
Hackle: Palest ginger tied in parachute

3. Pebble Caddis (Price)

DRESSING

Hook length: Up to 16mm
Thread: Brown
Abdomen: Cream floss coated in adhesive with small pieces of vermiculite stuck on (larger pieces can be added to sides to match natural)
Exposed body: Cream floss
Legs: Soft, short, brown hackle

Gipsywort
Lycopus europaeus (Plate 60)
Mint family (*Labiatae*)
(Water Horehound, Egyptian's Herb)

Flower head:	3–5mm long, white or pinkish flowers with tiny purple spots, carried in clusters of 10–20 at the bases of the leaves
Leaves:	Short-stalked, lance-shaped leaves carried in opposite pairs, the upper leaves being shallowly lobed

Flowering time:	July–September
Height:	Up to 1m
Habit:	Perennial
Habitat:	Watersides and damp places, reedbeds, edges of still and slow-flowing waters
Distribution:	Common throughout
General:	Gipsywort is a slightly hairy non-aromatic plant with some medicinal properties. A drug can be extracted from its upper parts that has a cardiotonic effect in calming palpitations and influencing sleep. Extracts from the plant are also useful in the treatment of malaria and fevers. The scientific name of gipsywort is derived from Greek words meaning 'wolf's foot' – a reference to the shape of the plant's roots. These roots contain juices, which, when extracted, can be used to make a dye useful in colouring silk and wool. Years ago wandering vagabonds would use this dye to stain their skin brown to give authenticity to their claims to be able to foretell the future. They seemed to have more credibility if their appearance looked foreign – hence the common term, 'Egyptian's Herb'

Mottled Sedge
Glyphotaelius pellucidus
(Plate 61)

This is a fairly distinctive-looking sedge resembling some of the moths that have markings imitating tree bark. It is another sedge that prefers areas of water with heavy vegetation. The larval case is very distinctive, being made from small leaves or cut pieces of larger ones. The leaves are held together with silken threads very similar to the pupation chambers of some terrestrial insects. Because of the nature and shape of the case it would be almost impossible to design an artificial match.

Larval case:	Whole or cut pieces of leaves
Size:	Up to 20mm
Adult:	
Size:	Up to 16mm
Abdomen:	Dark grey-green
Wings:	Distinctive shape to rear main wing, greyish with brown marks and patches
Habitat:	Still waters with vegetation
Distribution:	Reasonably well distributed
Time of day:	Mid-afternoon onwards
Time of year:	Late May–September

Dressings

1. Mottled Sedge

DRESSING

Hook length: Up to 16mm
Thread: Green
Abdomen: Olive seal's fur sub
Rib: Gold thread
Hackle: Abdomen palmered with well-marked Greenwell; head hackle dark-brown cock

2. Spent Partridge Caddis (Lawson)

DRESSING

Hook length: Up to 16mm
Thread: Green
Abdomen: Olive fur
Wing: Well-marked partridge tied at angle over abdomen
Hackle: Brown cock palmered over first third of peacock herl

Greater Bladderwort
Utricularia vulgaris (Plate 61)
Butterwort family
(*Lentribulariaceae*)

Flower head:	Bright yellow flowers up to 2cm long and held above water on long stalks. Each flower, which in appearance resembles a snapdragon, has two lipped sepals and petals and a short blunt spur
Leaves:	Finely divided submerged leaves with thread-like segments and numerous small bladders, 2–4mm wide on fine stalks from the leaf axis. Leaves are green or colourless
Flowering time:	July–August
Height:	Up to 40cm
Habit:	Native perennial
Habitat:	Lakes, ponds, ditches, stagnant or slow-flowing water
Distribution:	Localized throughout
General:	Greater Bladderwort is ▶

Plate 61

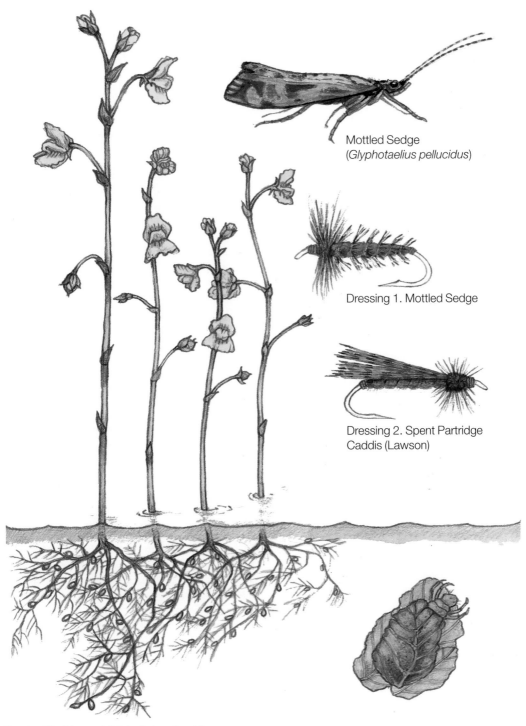

Mottled Sedge
(*Glyphotaelius pellucidus*)

Dressing 1. Mottled Sedge

Dressing 2. Spent Partridge
Caddis (Lawson)

Greater Bladderwort (*Utricularia vulgaris*)

Longhorn Sedge
Oecetis lacustris, ochracea (Plate 58)

This sedge species is found on still waters. The wings are long and narrow for their length, usually pale grey-yellow to pale silvery-brown. As the name would suggest, the antennae are very long, up to three times the body length. The sedge is common and emerges during daylight hours so can be very useful to the reservoir angler.

Larval case:	Slender, slightly curved, made from fine sand
Size:	Up to 17mm

Adult:	
Size:	Up to 13mm
Abdomen:	Pale green
Wings:	Slim, long, pale grey-yellow or pale silvery-brown
Habitat:	Still waters
Distribution:	Fairly common
Time of day:	After midday
Time of year:	June–September

Dressings

1. Grey Longhorn Sedge

DRESSING

Hook length: Up to 13mm
Thread: Green
Abdomen: Green floss
Rib: Green thread
Wing: Grey feather tips
Hackle: Grizzle
Antennae: Two pheasant tail fibres

2. Brown Longhorn Sedge

DRESSING

Hook length: Up to 13mm
Thread: Brown
Abdomen: Amber floss
Rib: Gold thread
Wing: Grey-brown feather tips
Hackle: Dull-brown cock
Antennae: Two hackle stalks

3. Sand Caddis

DRESSING

Hook length: Up to 17mm
Thread: Brown
Abdomen: Hare and sand-coloured fur mixed, dubbed and trimmed to shape
Rib: Gold wire
Exposed body: Brown or cream floss
Legs: Short partridge

Canadian Pondweed
Elodea canadensis (Plate 58)
Frogbit family (*Hydrocharitaceae*)
(Water Thyme)

Flower head:	Tiny, whitish flowers on long, thin stems. Petals are a translucent white, whilst the outer surfaces of the sepals are green with reddish markings. Male and female flowers grow on separate plants
Leaves:	Stalkless, dark green translucent leaves appearing in whorls of 3 around the stem. Lance-shaped with rounded or pointed tips

159

▶ a carnivorous free-floating aquatic plant with no real root system. *Utricularia* comes from the Latin *utriculus*, meaning 'small bag' or 'pouch' – a reference to the many small bladders present on the leaves. These bladders serve to keep the plant afloat in summer; when winter comes they fill with water and so the plant sinks to the bottom where it is protected from cold or frosts. The bladders also act as a means of trapping insects as a source of nutrients. Each bladder has a kind of lid which only opens inwards and is triggered by means of sensitive hairs. When any small insect brushes against these hairs the lid opens and the bladder stretches, sucking in water and the insect along with it. Digestive juices are then secreted into the bladder and the resultant nutrients absorbed back into the plant

Sand Fly
Rhyacophila dorsalis
(Plate 62)

At times it can be very useful to have a copy of both the adult and the larval stages of this sedge. It can be found in varying numbers throughout the fishing season, from late April through to early October. The adult appears from mid-afternoon well into the evening. The overall colour is orangey-brown and the antennae are slightly shorter than the length of wing. The larva is free-swimming and only constructs a rough case of small stones when ready to pupate. It is found in running water in most parts of the British Isles.

Larval case:	None
Size:	Up to 20mm

Adult:	
Size:	Up to 15mm
Abdomen:	Dull green
Wings:	Orangey-brown
Habitat:	Rivers and streams
Distribution:	Widespread and common
Time of day:	Mid-afternoon onwards
Time of year:	Late April–October

Dressings

1. Sand Fly

DRESSING

Hook length: Up to 15mm
Thread: Orange-brown
Abdomen: Sandy or yellow-green fur
Rib: Gold thread
Wing: Ginger cock fibres over abdomen
Hackle: Ginger cock

Plate 62

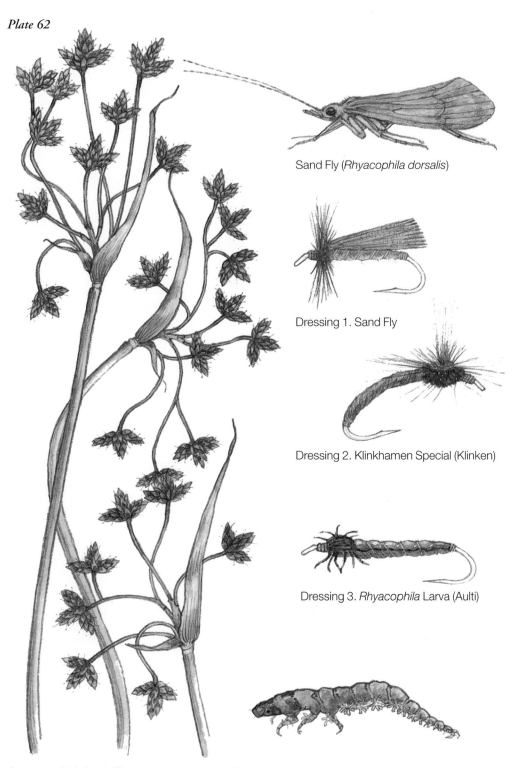

Sand Fly (*Rhyacophila dorsalis*)

Dressing 1. Sand Fly

Dressing 2. Klinkhamen Special (Klinken)

Dressing 3. *Rhyacophila* Larva (Aulti)

Common Club Rush (*Schoenoplectus lacustris*)

2. Klinkhamen Special (Klinken)

DRESSING

Hook length: Up to 16mm, curved
Thread: Yellow
Abdomen: Light-tan poly yarn
Thorax: Peacock herl
Wing: White poly yarn tied upright
Hackle: Chestnut or ginger cock

3. *Rhyacophila* Larva (Aulti)

DRESSING

Hook length: Up to 20mm
Thread: Brown
Abdomen: Olive antron with clear PVC strip over back
Rib: Yellow mono
Head cover: Partridge feather or similar
Legs: Ends of partridge fibres

Common Club Rush
Schoenoplectus lacustris
(Plate 62)

Flower head:	Spike is a dense, often branched mass of reddish-brown spikelets which have no petals but short, barbed bristles instead. They are carried on tall, stout, hairless stems which are rounded or triangular in section
Leaves:	Usually almost leafless although tufts of leaves may be produced by the creeping stem
Flowering time:	June–August
Height:	Up to 3m
Habit:	Perennial
Habitat:	Lakes, ponds, streams and riverbanks
Distribution:	Common
General:	The name comes from the Latin *lacustris*, meaning 'lake', and the Greek *schoinos* – 'a rush'. This plant used to grow in large beds in Norfolk until its near extinction there, and was harvested and used in the making of rush mats. Bullrush was the original common name, this now being the name of the plant originally known as the Reedmace. The confusion arose when the artist Alma-Tadema wrongly painted Reedmace instead of the Common Club Rush in *Moses in the Bullrushes*.

Silver Sedge
Odontocerum albicorne
(Plate 63)

The Silver or Grey Sedge is found in fast-running rivers and streams. The wings are fairly long and narrow, silver-grey in colour with darker veins. Antennae are longer than wing length. This sedge can be found on the wing throughout most of the day. The larva is another species that makes a fairly standard, slightly curved case from sand grains. Because of this standardization of certain case types identification of some species in the larval stage is almost impossible.

Larval case:	Curved, slightly tapered, made from sand grains
Size:	Up to 20mm
Adult:	
Size:	Up to 17mm
Abdomen:	Grey-black

Plate 63

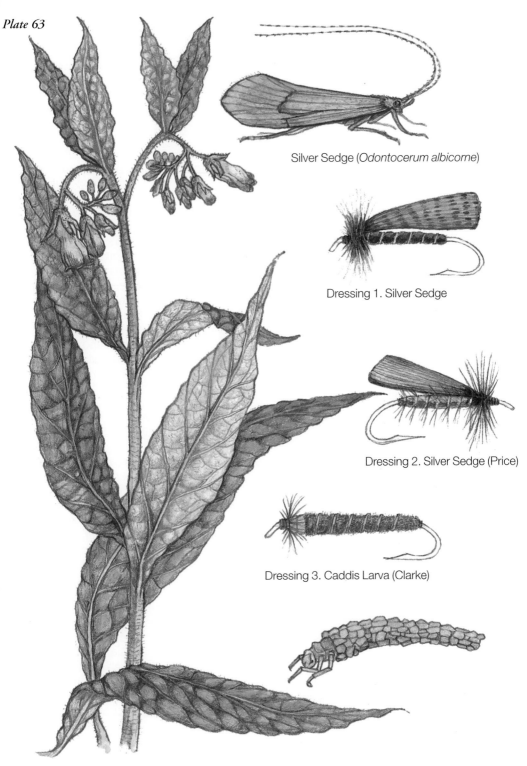

Silver Sedge (*Odontocerum albicorne*)

Dressing 1. Silver Sedge

Dressing 2. Silver Sedge (Price)

Dressing 3. Caddis Larva (Clarke)

Comfrey (*Symphytum officinale*)

Wings:	Silvery grey
Habitat:	Faster-running streams and rivers
Distribution:	Fairly widespread
Time of day:	Throughout the day
Time of year:	June–September

Dressings

1. Silver Sedge

DRESSING

Hook length: Up to 17mm
Thread: Black
Abdomen: Dark-grey fur
Rib: Gold thread
Wing: Grey mallard fibres tied over back
Hackle: Grizzle or well-marked badger cock

2. Silver Sedge (Price)

DRESSING

Hook length: Up to 17mm
Thread: Grey or black
Abdomen: Grey floss
Rib: Silver wire
Wing: Coot or grey feathers tied over the back
Hackle: Palmered ginger tied full at the head

3. Caddis Larva (Clarke)

DRESSING

Hook length: Up to 17mm
Thread: Brown
Abdomen: Bronze or sandy-coloured peacock herl
Rib: Copper wire
Exposed body: Fawn-coloured yarn
Legs: Short honey hen hackle

Comfrey
Symphytum officinale (Plate 63)
Comfrey family (*Boraginaceae*)
(Knitbone, Boneset)

Flower head:	Cream, white, mauve or pink bell-shaped flowers, 12–18mm long in coiled sprays curving downwards, similar to a bishop's crozier. Flower heads rise from the joint between leaves and stem
Leaves:	Lower leaves are hairy and long-stalked, lance-shaped and with smooth margins. Upper leaves are stalkless and the margin continues down the stem to form a wing. When crushed, the leaves give off a pleasant smell
Flowering time:	May–September
Height:	Up to 1.5m
Habit:	Native perennial
Habitat:	Damp places, riverbanks, ditches, wet woods and streams
Distribution:	Common – less so in Scotland and Ireland
General:	A tall, robust, hairy plant often found growing in big, bushy clumps at the water's edge. The name 'comfrey' is taken from Latin *confere*, meaning 'to join'. *Symphytus* is Greek for growing together of bones and *phyton* is a plant, alluding to the plant's usefulness in the setting of broken bones – hence its other common names of Knitbone or Boneset. Other ailments for which comfrey was used ▶

▶ medicinally were ulcers and back pain, and the roots and leaves were said to bring out bruising when applied as a poultice. Comfrey can also be used as a food source as it may be eaten as a vegetable similar to spinach or fried in batter. The root can be used as a coffee substitute when dried and ground. It also has a part to play in organic gardening as it makes an excellent liquid manure and can be used both in composting and as a mulch for plants

Larval case: None, builds galleries on rocks
Size: Larva up to 11mm, galleries up to 40mm

Adult:
Size: Up to 8mm
Abdomen: Grey to reddish-brown
Wings: Red-brown
Habitat: Still and running water
Distribution: Widespread and fairly abundant
Time of day: After midday
Time of year: May–October

Small Red Sedge
Tinodes waeneri (Plate 64)

This sedge is very well known to fly fishermen because of the patterns and writings of G. E. M. Skues. It is reasonably small and, as the name suggests, its wings are a red-brown colour. The family to which *Tinodes* belongs, *Psychomyidae*, builds narrow, tubular, silk galleries on rocks. The silken tunnels are usually camouflaged with small pieces of sand or vegetable particles taken from the surrounding area. They are to be found in still and running water and the species is both widespread and fairly abundant. There is no pattern for the larva.

Dressings

1. Little Red Sedge (Skues)

DRESSING
Hook length: Up to 8mm
Thread: Orange
Abdomen: Dark hare's fur
Rib: Gold wire
Wing: Red-brown partridge over back
Hackle: Red cock palmered length of body, full at head

2. Red Sedge

DRESSING
Hook length: Up to 8mm
Thread: Orange
Abdomen: Grey rabbit's fur
Rib: Silver wire
Wing: Grey mallard
Hackle: Red cock

Plate 64

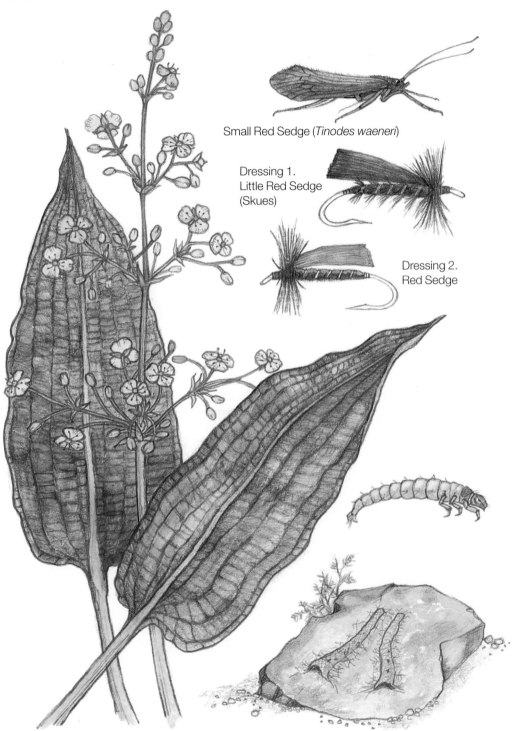

Small Red Sedge (*Tinodes waeneri*)

Dressing 1.
Little Red Sedge
(Skues)

Dressing 2.
Red Sedge

Water Plantain (*Alisma plantago-aquatica*)

Water Plantain
Alisma plantago-aquatica
(Plate 64)
Water Plantain family
(*Alismataceae*)

Flower head:	Flowers are made up of 3 delicate white petals, tinged with yellow at the base and carried in whorls up the stem. Each branch is divided into smaller whorls
Leaves:	Pale green leaves with a marked patterning of veins, oval in shape and on long, spongy stalks, forming a basal rosette
Flowering time:	June–August
Height:	Up to 1m
Habit:	Native perennial
Habitat:	Margins of stagnant or slow-flowing waters and wet, muddy places
Distribution:	Common except Scotland
General:	One of five species of Water Plantains, all unrelated to other plantains, and only called so because of the similarity of their leaves. The tiny, delicate flowers remain closed all morning and do not open until the afternoon but are already closed again by early evening. Its scientific name *Alisma* comes from the Greek name for a water plant

Small Silver Sedge
Lepidostoma hirtum
(Plate 65)

The Small Silver Sedge is fairly widespread but can be very localized. The shape of the wings gives it a short, stout appearance. The body and wings are usually grey-brown. It is found mostly in running water from May to late August. The larval case is fairly unusual in that it is almost square in section and made up mostly of cut vegetation.

Larval case:	Square in section, made from cut leaves, etc
Size:	Up to 16mm
Adult:	
Size:	Up to 10mm
Abdomen:	Grey-brown
Wings:	Grey-brown
Habitat:	Mostly running water
Distribution:	Widespread but localized
Time of day:	Evening
Time of year:	May–August

Dressings

1. Small Silver Sedge

DRESSING
Hook length: Up to 10mm
Thread: Green
Abdomen: Pale grey-brown fur
Rib: Green thread
Wing: Grey feather over body
Hackle: Ginger cock

Plate 65

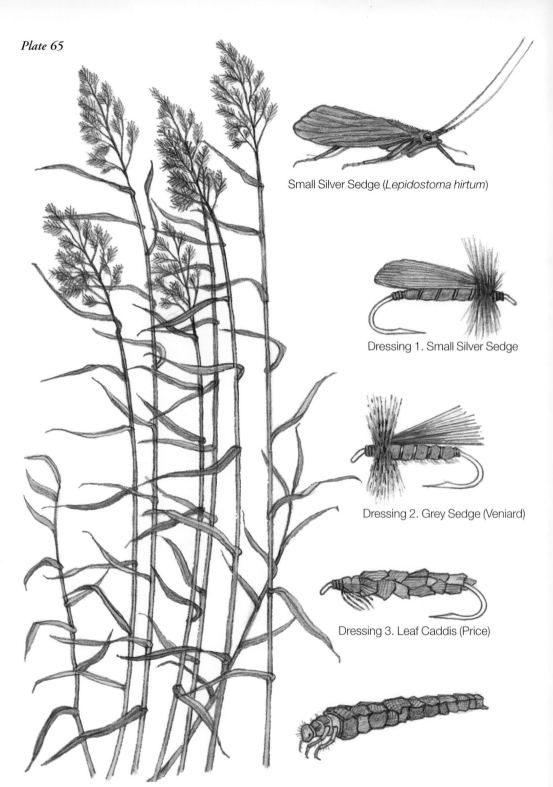

Small Silver Sedge (*Lepidostoma hirtum*)

Dressing 1. Small Silver Sedge

Dressing 2. Grey Sedge (Veniard)

Dressing 3. Leaf Caddis (Price)

Common Reed (*Phragmites australis*)

2. Grey Sedge (Veniard)

DRESSING

Hook length: Up to 10mm
Thread: Green
Abdomen: Grey seal's fur sub
Rib: Silver wire
Wing: Grey squirrel tail fibres
Hackle: Grizzle cock

3. Leaf Caddis (Price)

DRESSING

Hook length: Up to 16mm
Thread: Brown
Abdomen: Pale-green floss with cut pieces of natural and coloured raffia stuck on
Exposed body: Pale-green floss
Legs: Red hen or small partridge

Common Reed
Phragmites australis (Plate 65)
Grass family (*Graminae*)

Flower head:	Large, soft, upright flower head made up of purplish or brownish spikes. Each floret has soft, white hairs surrounding it which assist in wind dispersing of the seed
Leaves:	Small, greyish-green leaves, the base of which forms a sheath around the stem. Where the base joins the stem there is also a dense fringe of short hairs
Flowering time:	July–September
Height:	Up to 3m
Habit:	Perennial
Habitat:	Edges of rivers, lakes and marshes, fens
Distribution:	Common

General: The Common Reed, which is the tallest of Britain's grasses, forms itself very rapidly into huge beds at the sides of rivers and lakes. It has a very tough root system which can successfully spread over mud, and once established it is very difficult to get rid of. The stems, when harvested, are used in the production of cellulose and paper pulp, and also make ideal thatching material. At one time Common Reeds were planted along ditches to form fences, hence the name *Phragmites*, taken from the Greek *phragma* – a 'partition' or 'screen'

Small Yellow Sedge
Psychomyia pusilla (Plate 66)

This is one of the smallest sedges of interest to the fisherman. It is fairly plain, being an overall fawny-brown-yellow colour with short, stout antennae. Found mostly in running water, it can also be found around the edges of stony lakes. The larvae, like those of *Tinodes*, the Small Red Sedge, form galleries on rocks in fairly shallow water. Adults are found on the wing from June to September, mostly from early evening onwards.

Larval case:	None, they live in tubular galleries
Size:	Up to 9mm
Adult:	
Size:	Up to 6mm
Abdomen:	Brownish-yellow

177

Plate 66

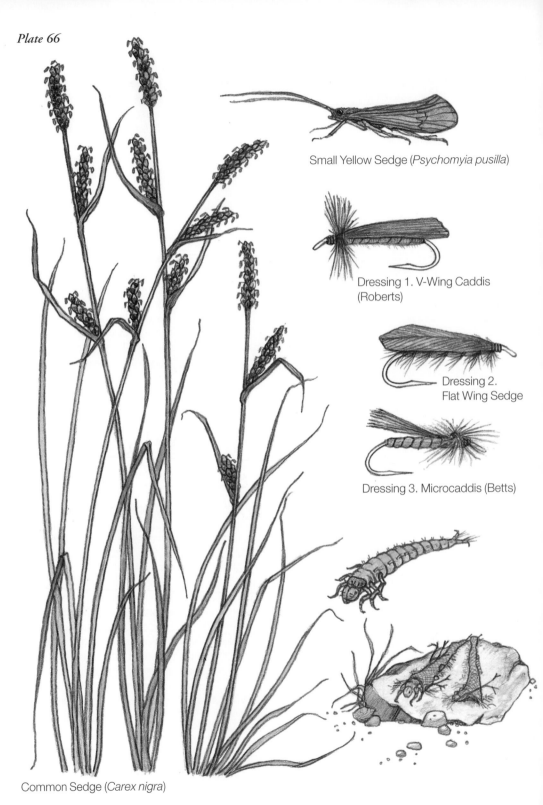

Small Yellow Sedge (*Psychomyia pusilla*)

Dressing 1. V-Wing Caddis (Roberts)

Dressing 2. Flat Wing Sedge

Dressing 3. Microcaddis (Betts)

Common Sedge (*Carex nigra*)

Wings:	Fawn to brownish-yellow
Habitat:	Running and still waters
Distribution:	Widespread and reasonably abundant
Time of day:	Towards evening
Time of year:	June–September

Dressings

1. V-wing Caddis (Roberts)

DRESSING

Hook length: Up to 6mm
Thread: Pale brown
Abdomen: Brown-yellow poly dubbing or similar
Rib: Thread
Wing: Rolled quill from a pale yellow-brown feather
Hackle: Dull, pale ginger

2. Flat Wing Sedge

DRESSING

Hook length: Up to 6mm
Thread: Yellow-brown
Abdomen: Yellow-brown fur; a palmered pale ginger cock is run the length of the body with the underside fibres trimmed short
Wing: One or two feathers tied in a tent shape over the body, pale yellow-brown

3. Microcaddis (Betts)

DRESSING

Hook length: Up to 6mm
Thread: Yellow-brown
Abdomen: Fine yellow-brown fur or similar
Rib: Thread
Wing: Pale-ginger hackle fibres
Hackle: Pale-ginger cock tied parachute

Common Sedge
Carex nigra (Plate 66)
Sedge family

Flower head:	A blackish spike of very small scales each enclosing either a stamen or an ovary and carried at the end of triangular stems
Leaves:	Very narrow grass-like leaves, sometimes longer than the stems. In dry conditions the leaf margins may be curled up
Flowering time:	May–July
Height:	Up to 80cm
Habit:	Perennial
Habitat:	Wet, grassy areas or beside water
Distribution:	Common
General:	This clump-forming, grass-like plant is one of seventy-five species of sedge found in Britain. It has a preference for acid soils and may sometimes be seen growing as an ornamental. The dark-coloured, wind-pollinated spikes are made up of only either male or female flowers. The scientific name *nigra*, meaning 'black', alludes to the colour of these spikes, whilst *Carex* is taken from the Greek *kairo* – 'to cut' – a reference to the sharp edges of the leaves

Welshman's Button
Sericostoma personatum
(Plate 67)

One of the fascinating things about fly fishing is the history of the subject and particularly the design and the naming of flies. This sedge was named by F. M. Halford but the name was originally applied to a beetle. Before this time the fly was known as the Dun Cut. The fly appears around early June and on into September. It is not, as its name implies, a fly confined to Wales, but can be found on rivers and streams, and less frequently on lakes, throughout the country. Hatches can be fairly heavy at any time during the day. The wings are hairy and a dark grey or rich brown. The antennae are approximately as long as the wings. Larval cases are again of the slightly curved sand grain type.

Larval case: Made of sand grains, curved and tapered
Size: Up to 18mm

Adult:
Size: Up to 15mm
Abdomen: Greyish-green
Wings: Angular, grey-brown to rich-brown
Habitat: Mostly streams and rivers, occasionally lakes
Distribution: Reasonably distributed
Time of day: Throughout the day
Time of year: June–September

Dressings

1. Fluttering Caddis (Wright)

DRESSING

Hook length: Up to 15mm
Thread: Brown
Abdomen: Cock pheasant tail fibres
Rib: Gold wire
Wing: Brown cock fibres over body
Hackle: Brown cock

2. Welshman's Button

DRESSING

Hook length: Up to 15mm
Thread: Brown
Abdomen: Peacock herl with palmered brown cock cut short
Rib: Gold wire
Wing: Brown deer hair
Hackle: Brown cock

3. Sand Caddis (Price)

DRESSING

Hook length: Up to 18mm
Thread: Brown
Abdomen: Cream floss coated with adhesive and covered in sand
Exposed body: Cream or green floss
Legs: Brown hen, short

Plate 67

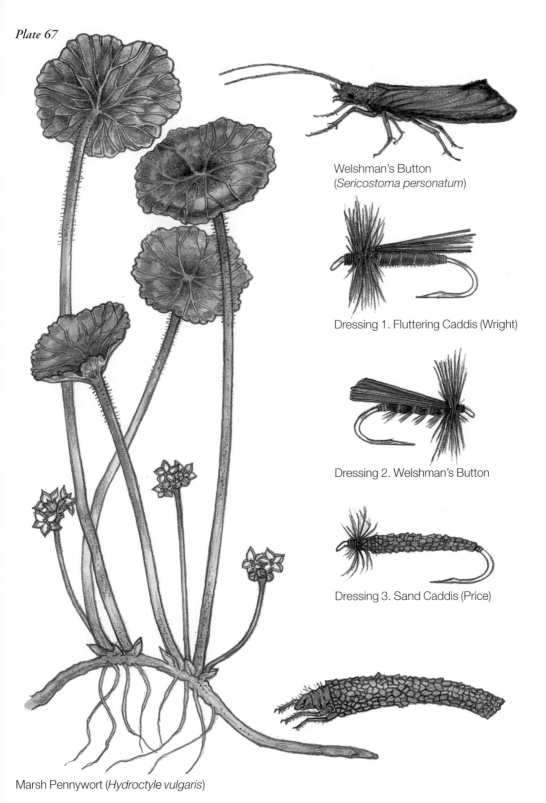

Welshman's Button
(*Sericostoma personatum*)

Dressing 1. Fluttering Caddis (Wright)

Dressing 2. Welshman's Button

Dressing 3. Sand Caddis (Price)

Marsh Pennywort (*Hydroctyle vulgaris*)

Marsh Pennywort
Hydroctyle vulgaris **(Plate 67)**
Carrot family (*Umbellifereae*)
(White Rot, Sheep Rot)

Flower head: Numerous small, greenish-white flowers carried on short stalks in an umbrella-shaped head growing from the leaf axis
Leaves: Bluish-green leaves, round in shape, carried on stalks growing from the middle of the underside of the leaves. Edges are notched
Flowering time: June–August
Height: Up to 25cm
Habit: Native perennial
Habitat: Bogs, fens, marshes, ditches, banks, shallow water
Distribution: Common
General: Marsh Pennywort is a prostrate creeping plant often found floating in shallow water. The name Pennywort comes from the round shape of its penny-like leaves. Another of its common names – Sheep Rot – derives from the once-held belief that marsh pennywort did cause rotting in sheep's feet; it has since been shown the disease is actually caused by the liver fluke, which occurs in the same places as the plant

Yellow Spotted Sedge
Philopotamus montanus
(Plate 68)

This is a fly usually found in the higher, swift mountain streams. Similar sedges are found in more varied locations but these usually have darker markings. A general, similarly marked artificial should cover most requirements. The larva constructs nets, and in this stage of development the sedge is of no interest to the fisherman.

Larval case: Larva constructs nets
Size: Up to 22mm

Adult:
Size: 10–14mm
Abdomen: Dark red-brown
Wings: Usually dark brown with yellow spots but variations can occur with darker markings
Habitat: Boulder-strewn, fast-flowing streams
Distribution: Common and widespread in certain locations
Time of day: After midday
Time of year: June–September

Dressings

1. Spotted Sedge

DRESSING

Hook length: 14mm
Thread: Deep yellow
Abdomen: Rich-brown fur with palmered ginger hackle, very short
Wing: Light raffia, treated and marked with pen
Hackle: Ginger cock

Plate 68

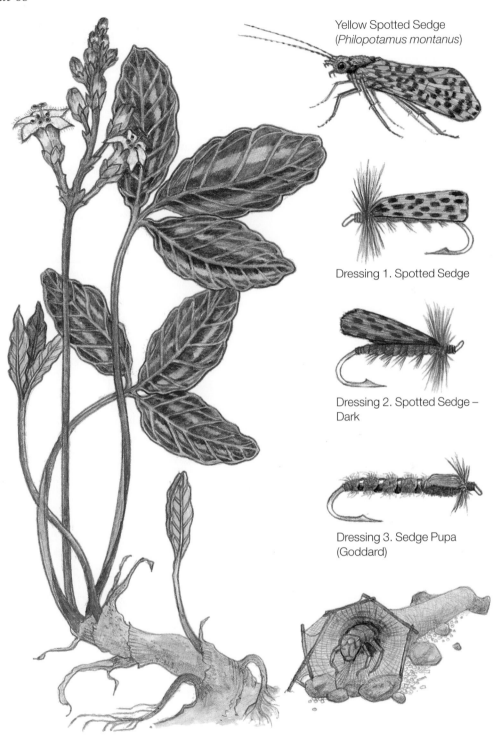

Yellow Spotted Sedge
(*Philopotamus montanus*)

Dressing 1. Spotted Sedge

Dressing 2. Spotted Sedge –
Dark

Dressing 3. Sedge Pupa
(Goddard)

Bog Bean (*Menyanthes trifoliata*)

2. Spotted Sedge Dark

DRESSING

Hook length: 10–14mm
Thread: Brown
Abdomen: Red-brown fur with palmered red-brown hackle, short
Wing: Well-marked speckled hen feather
Hackle: Red-brown cock

3. Sedge Pupa (Goddard)

DRESSING

Hook length: 10–14mm
Thread: Brown
Abdomen: Brown seal's fur sub
Rib: Silver tinsel
Thorax: Dark-brown turkey herl
Wingcase: Pale-brown feather fibre
Legs: Brown hen hackle, short

Bog Bean
Menyanthes trifoliata (Plate 68)
Bogbean family (*Menyanthaceae*)
(Buck Bean, Marsh Trefoil,
Goatsbeard)

Flower head: Held above water and consisting of 10–15 pinkish buds each opening out to reveal a whitish, star-shaped flower tinged pink on outer surface. Flowers are 14–16mm across, with 5 sepals and 5 petals, the latter densely covered with white shaggy hairs on their inner surface (hence the name 'Goatsbeard')

Leaves: Large and trifoliate like clover and held above water on long tubular stalks. Each leaf consists of 3 thickish, leathery, stalkless leaflets, dark green in colour and with a pale prominent midrib and untoothed margins

Fruit: Many-seeded egg-shaped capsule

Flowering time: May–July

Height: Up to 30cm

Habit: Perennial

Habitat: Bogs and shallow waters, pond and lake edges

Distribution: Common throughout Britain, can be abundant

General: This common native perennial is often seen in ornamental gardens. It cannot grow in deep water and has a preference for rich, muddy sites, allowing its thick underground stems to creep over and colonize large areas. Its scientific name is derived from Greek – *men* meaning 'moon' or 'month', and *anthos* meaning 'flower' – references both to duration of its flower and use as a treatment for menstrual pain. Common name 'Bog Bean' or 'Buck Bean' is a derivative of the German *Bocksbohnen* – Goat's Beans. In Germany, an extract of Bog Bean was often prescribed as a general tonic. The Irish believed it purified the blood and cured boils. Its bitter leaves were used to flavour beer and for use in herbal cigarettes. Powdered root of Bog Bean was used as a kind of flour by the Inuit peoples of North America. Bog Bean has been greatly admired down the centuries by botanists and herbalists alike

Sedge Pupae/Emergers

The point of transposition from pupa to adult sedge is, as in the same stage in the upwinged flies' life cycle, of great importance to the fisherman. At this moment the fly changes from one 'type' of creature to another, and the escape from the pupal shuck, the breaking free of water surface tension, the adult struggling to become airborne, all leave the sedge at the mercy of the trout. Once again the fly designer is faced with a compromise stage of caddis pupa and the emerging adult. Most artificials have some form of pupal stage designed for the rear half of the hook with the front half dressed to reveal emerging wings, legs and antennae.

When ready to pupate, the caddis larva will anchor the case to some small stones or other firm objects with silk threads; free-living larvae form a rough silken shelter. The larva then spins a cocoon and pupation takes place. The free pupa can now, with the use of its legs, crawl or swim to the bankside or water surface, where transformation to adult can take place. The adult can fly away almost immediately but the wings, being 'thicker' than those of the upwinged flies, usually need a time to 'harden'. This usually takes place after the initial flight. Most of the sedge pupa/emerger patterns can be adapted to particular species by altering the size and colour.

Dressings (Plates 69 and 70)

1. Emergent Sparkle Pupa (LaFontaine)

DRESSING

Hook length: Up to 15mm
Thread: Brown
Abdomen: Sandy-coloured sparkle yarn, some fibres tied in at the head and tail to form the 'bulge' of the hatching body
Wing: Natural deer hair over body
Head: Brown feather fibres

2. Hatching Sedge Pupa (Roberts)

DRESSING

Hook length: Up to 16mm
Thread: Orange
Abdomen: Orange-brown seal's fur sub
Rib: Gold tinsel
Hackle: Brown partridge
Head: 'Muddler' deer hair

Plate 69

Sedge Pupae/Emergers

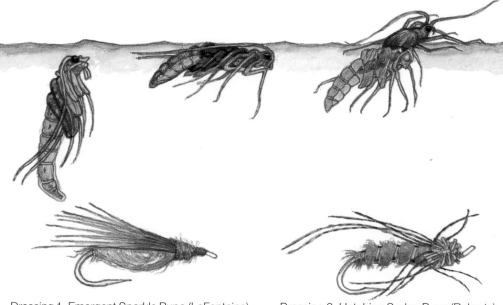

Dressing 1. Emergent Sparkle Pupa (LaFontaine)

Dressing 2. Hatching Sedge Pupa (Roberts)

Dressing 4. Swannundaze Sedge Pupa (Price)

Dressing 3. Longhorn Sedge Pupa (Walker)

Dressing 5. Sedge Pupa (Kendall)

Dressing 6. Latex Pupa (Fogg)

Dressing 7. Caddis Pupa (Wootton)

Dressing 8. Fur Caddis Pupa (Jorgensen)

3. Longhorn Sedge Pupa (Walker)

DRESSING

Hook length: Up to 16mm
Thread: Pale yellow
Abdomen: First third brown wool, last two thirds amber wool
Rib: Oval gold tinsel
Hackle: Brown partridge
Antennae: Cock pheasant herls

4. Swannundaze Sedge Pupa (Price)

DRESSING

Hook length: Up to 16mm
Thread: Brown
Abdomen: Red floss covered with amber swannundaze
Rib: Peacock herl between layers of abdomen
Thorax: Brown fur
Wingcase: Cock pheasant fibres over thorax
Legs: Brown partridge
Antennae: Cock pheasant herls

5. Sedge-Pupa (Kendall)

DRESSING

Hook length: Up to 16mm
Thread: Brown
Abdomen: A mix of antron and seal's fur sub in ginger
Rib: Clear polythene
Legs: Partridge fibres
Thorax: Ginger-brown seal's fur sub
Emerging wing: Ginger feather fibres to shape
Antennae: Bronze mallard

6. Latex Pupa (Fogg)

DRESSING

Hook length: Up to 14mm
Thread: Brown
Abdomen: Lime-green floss covered with a full rib of Latex strip
Thorax: Brown herl
Hackle: Brown hen

7. Caddis Pupa (Wootton)

DRESSING

Hook length: Up to 16mm
Thread: Brown
Abdomen: Dubbed green SLF
Emerging wing: Raffene cut to shape
Hackle: Brown hen
Thorax: Brown SLF
Antennae: Bronze mallard

8. Fur Caddis Pupa (Jorgensen)

DRESSING

Hook length: Up to 16mm
Thread: Brown
Abdomen: Brown fur formed tight round hook with tying thread
Emerging wing: Two small mallard slips
Hackle: Brown partridge
Thorax: Brown fur

9. Gongi Sedge Pupa (Klinken)

DRESSING

Hook length: Up to 16mm
Thread: Green
Abdomen: Ginger fur with Latex over
Rib: Ginger hackle palmered and cut very short
Wing: Brown hackle fibres
Thorax: Dark-green seal's fur sub

12. Sedge Pupa (Cove)

DRESSING

Hook length: Up to 15mm
Thread: Olive
Abdomen: Pale-green seal's fur sub, the back covered with pheasant tail fibres
Thorax: Rabbit fur picked out

10. Ascending Sedge (Edwards)

DRESSING

Hook length: Up to 14mm
Thread: Brown
Abdomen: Pale-green antron under a back of green swan fibres
Rib: Gold wire
Emerging wing: Dark brown-black raffene either side
Thorax: Brown seal's fur sub
Legs: Cock pheasant herls
Antennae: Dyed mallard fibres

13. Mono Sedge Pupa (Roberts)

DRESSING

Hook length: Up to 13mm
Thread: Green
Abdomen: Green thread covered with clear nylon mono
Hackle: Brown partridge
Thorax: Peacock herl

11. Deep Sparkle Pupa (LaFontaine)

DRESSING

Hook length: Up to 15mm
Thread: Orange
Abdomen: A mix of sparkle yarn and squirrel fur in cream, orange, red and olive. This is covered in a loose 'bulge' of clear olive and orange, tied in at head and rear of body
Legs: Partridge
Head: Dark-orange marabou

14. Sedge Pupa (Goddard)

DRESSING

Hook length: Up to 15mm
Thread: Brown
Abdomen: Orange seal's fur sub
Rib: Silver tinsel
Thorax: Brown feather herls
Emerging wing: Pale feather fibres
Hackle: Pale-ginger hen

Plate 70

Dressing 10. Ascending Sedge (Edwards)

Dressing 9. Gongi Sedge Pupa (Klinken)

Dressing 12. Sedge Pupa (Cove)

Dressing 11. Deep Sparkle Pupa (LaFontaine)

Dressing 14. Sedge Pupa (Goddard)

Dressing 13. Mono Sedge Pupa (Roberts)

Dressing 16. Sedge Emerger (Jardine)

Dressing 15. Sedge Pupa (Fraser)

Dressing 18. Amber Pupa (Bell)

Dressing 17. Hatching Sedge Pupa (Goddard)

Dressing 20. Longhorn Emerging Pupa

Dressing 19. Small Green Pupa (Jardine)

15. Sedge Pupa (Fraser)

DRESSING

Hook length: Up to 15mm
Thread: Brown
Abdomen: Amber seal's fur sub
Rib: Yellow floss
Thorax: Yellow seal's fur sub
Wingcase: Hen pheasant fibres
Emerging wing: Tips of wingcase tied in either side

18. Amber Pupa (Bell)

DRESSING

Hook length: Up to 15mm
Thread: Yellow
Abdomen: Amber seal's fur sub
Rib: Gold wire
Wingcase: Brown feather fibres over body
Thorax: Orange seal's fur sub
Legs: Honey hen hackle fibres

16. Sedge Emerger (Jardine)

DRESSING

Hook length: Up to 12mm
Thread: Brown
Abdomen: Brown rabbit's fur
Rib: Gold wire
Emerging wing: Mallard
Legs: Partridge
Thorax: Rabbit's fur picked out

19. Small Green Pupa (Jardine)

DRESSING

Hook length: Up to 12mm
Thread: Brown
Abdomen: Insect green dubbing
Rib: Gold wire
Emerging wing: Grey mallard
Legs: Brown partridge
Thorax: Brown rabbit's fur

17. Hatching Sedge Pupa (Goddard)

DRESSING

Hook length: Up to 14mm
Thread: Orange
Abdomen: Orange seal's fur sub
Rib: Silver wire
Wing: Grey mallard slips
Legs: Brown partridge
Antennae: Brown mallard herls

20. Longhorn Emerging Pupa

DRESSING

Hook length: Up to 15mm
Thread: Brown
Abdomen: Orange-brown seal's fur sub
Rib: Clear polythene or mono
Emerging wing: Brown feather fibres
Legs: Partridge fibres
Antennae: Mallard fibres

PART 3

Likely Suspects

If the identification of a fly is not clear from the individual illustrations and remarks on the full-page colour sections, then here is a more detailed analysis of a fly's salient features.

When we catch a specimen, the first question to answer – particularly with the upwinged flies – is what sex is the fly we are examining? In the upwings, colour differences occur between male and female, particularly in their abdomens; eyes and wings also show variations.

It is a reasonably simple matter to sex the fly – for most species some form of hand lens is essential. This will also help in the study of the (in some specimens) minute rear wings. Below are the main differences in sexing your sample fly. The eyes of the female are in general smaller than the male's. The male's abdomen ends in a pair of forceps or claspers, which are used to grasp the female in the mating flight.

Once the sex of the fly has been determined we can move onto the charts. These are arranged in fly size order, starting with the large Mayfly and going down to the smallest, the *Caenis*. Size is only a guide and the other criteria – rear wings, colour, eyes, habitat – should be considered in the final determination.

Female

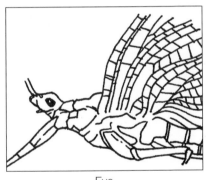

Eye

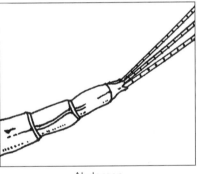

Abdomen

Male

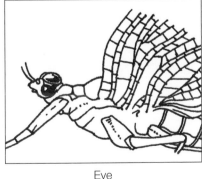

Eye

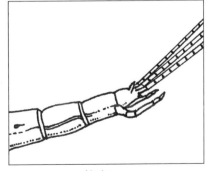

Abdomen

Basic differences in Male and Female *Ephemeroptera*

Key to Upwing Identification

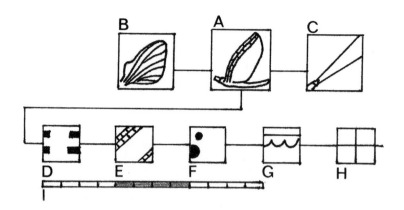

Box **A** shows actual size of natural.

Box **B** shows magnified shape of rear wing. If the box is empty there is no rear wing.

Box **C** shows number of tails.

Box **D** shows abdomen colour: female at top, male at bottom.

Box **E** shows colour of main wing and where cross veins are sharp or blurred.

Box **F** shows colour of eyes: female at top, male at bottom.

Box **G** shows type of habitat: flat line = still water, wavy line = reasonable flow, pointed line = fast flow; type of bottom: rocky or silt.

Box **H** shows distribution: one line = rare, cross = reasonably scarce or localised, cross and diagonal lines = common and widespread.

Box **I** shows months of year to expect natural when shaded in.

Colours

b = brown bl = black bu = blue c = cream d = dark f = fawn
g = green gr = grey o = olive or = orange p = pale r = red
s = silver y = yellow

Upwings 1

Mayfly

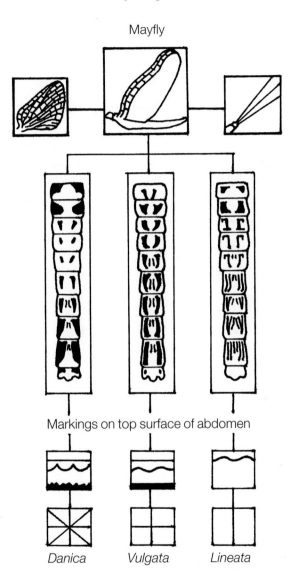

Markings on top surface of abdomen

Danica   Vulgata   Lineata

Upwings 2

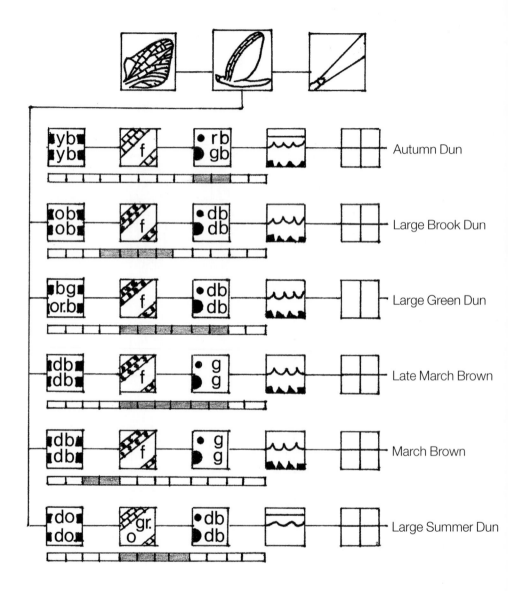

Autumn Dun

Large Brook Dun

Large Green Dun

Late March Brown

March Brown

Large Summer Dun

Upwings 3

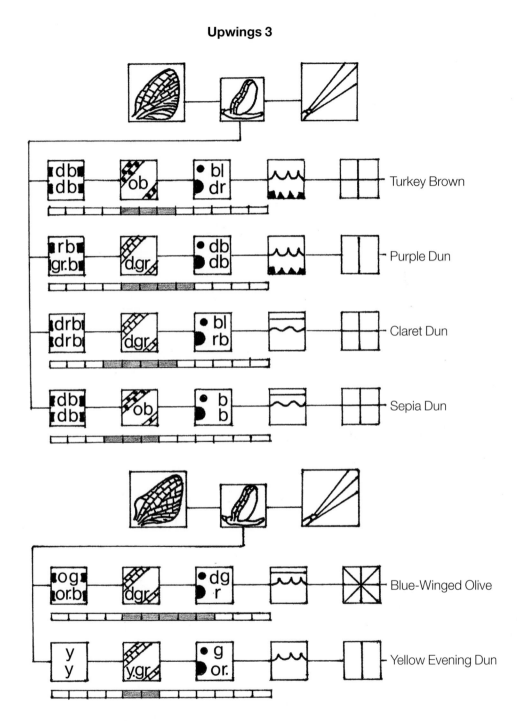

Turkey Brown

Purple Dun

Claret Dun

Sepia Dun

Blue-Winged Olive

Yellow Evening Dun

Upwings 4

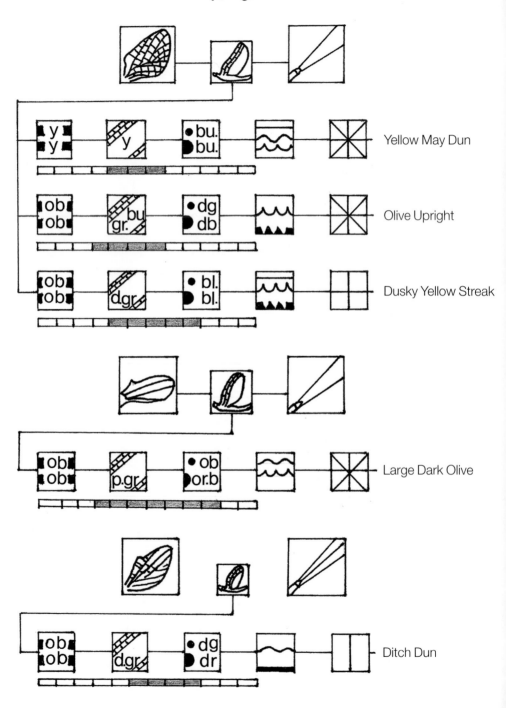

Yellow May Dun

Olive Upright

Dusky Yellow Streak

Large Dark Olive

Ditch Dun

Upwings 5

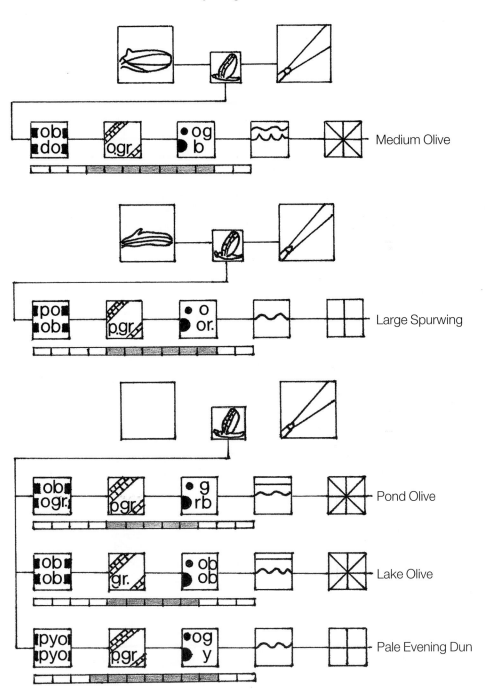

Medium Olive

Large Spurwing

Pond Olive

Lake Olive

Pale Evening Dun

Upwings 6

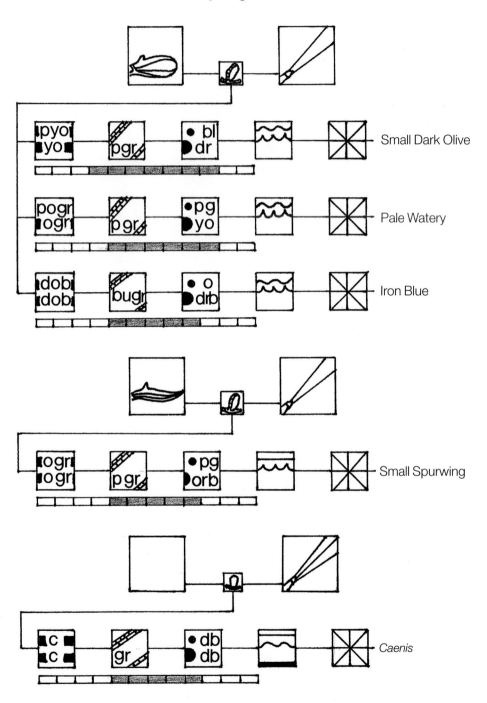

Small Dark Olive

Pale Watery

Iron Blue

Small Spurwing

Caenis

Key to Sedge Identification

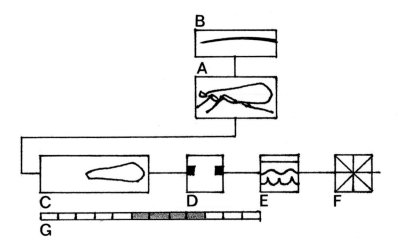

Box **A** shows actual size of natural.

Box **B** shows actual size of antennae.

Box **C** shows shape and colour of wings.

Box **D** shows abdomen colour.

Box **E** shows type of habitat: flat line = still water, wavy line = reasonable flow, pointed line = fast flow.

Box **F** shows distribution: one line = rare, cross = reasonably scarce or localised, cross and diagonal lines = common and widespread

Box **G** shows months of year to expect natural when shaded in

Colours
b = brown bl = black bu = blue c = cream d = dark f = fawn
g = green gr = grey o = olive or = orange p = pale r = red
s = silver y = yellow

Sedge 1

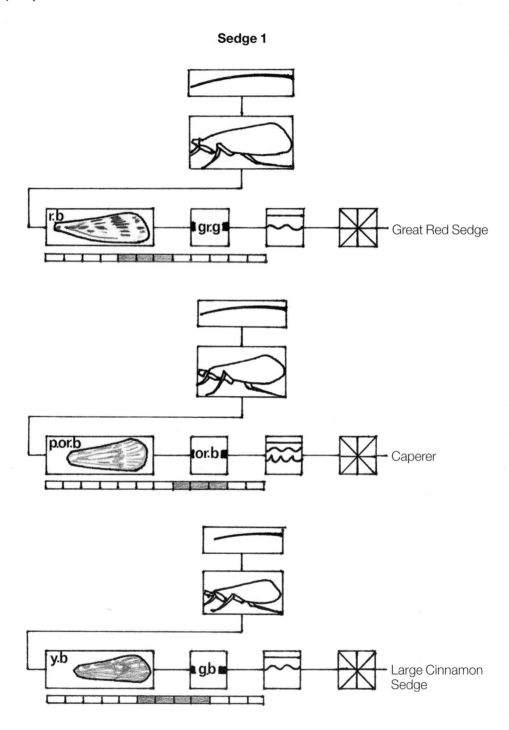

Sedge 2

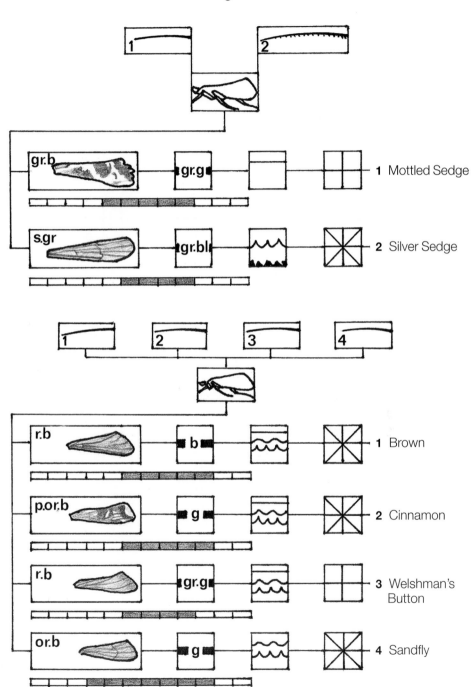

1 Mottled Sedge

2 Silver Sedge

1 Brown

2 Cinnamon

3 Welshman's Button

4 Sandfly

Sedge 3

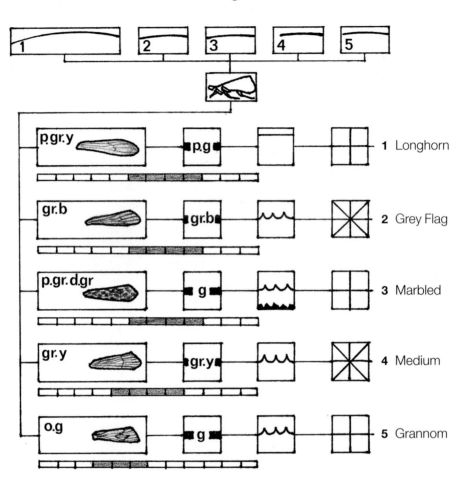

1 Longhorn

2 Grey Flag

3 Marbled

4 Medium

5 Grannom

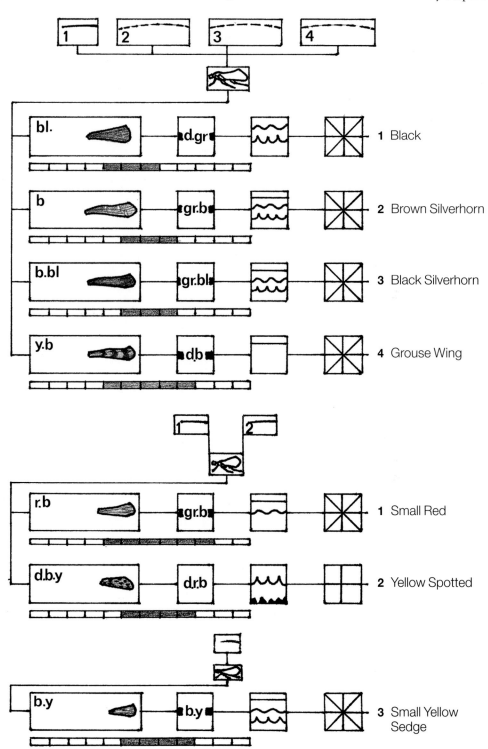

1 Black

2 Brown Silverhorn

3 Black Silverhorn

4 Grouse Wing

1 Small Red

2 Yellow Spotted

3 Small Yellow
Sedge

Bibliography

Aichele & Schwegler, *Wild Flowers of Britain and Europe*, Hamlyn

Akeroyd, J., *Encyclopedia of Wild Flowers*, Dempsey Parr, 1999

Back, P., *The Illustrated Herbal*, Hamlyn, 1987

Chinery, M., *Insects*, Harper Collins, 1994

Clarke, B. & Goddard, J., *The Trout and the Fly*, Benn, 1980

Courtney Williams, A., *A Dictionary of Trout Flies*, A & C Black, 1949

Culpeper, N., *The Complete Herbal*, Cleave & Son, 1826

Dawes, M., *Fly Tier's Manual*, Collins Willow 1985

Elliott, J. & Humpesch, *British Ephemeroptera*, Freshwater Biological Association, 1983

Elliott, Humpesch, Macan, *Larvae of British Ephemeroptera*, Freshwater Biological Association, 1988

Engelhardt, W., *Pond Life*, Burke, 1964

Fitter, R. & Manuel, R., *Freshwater Life*, Collins, 1986

Goddard, J., *Trout Fly Recognition*, A & C Black, 1983

Goddard, J., *Waterside Guide*, Collins Willow, 1997

Grey-Wilson, C., *Wild Flowers of Britain and Northwest Europe*, Dorling Kindersley, 1995

Harris, J., *An Angler's Entomology*, Collins, 1952

Jardine, C., *Dark Pools*, Crowood Press, 1991

Jardine, C., *Fly Fishing*, Dorling Kindersley, 1994

Martin, W. K., *The Concise British Flora in Colour*, Ebury Press, 1965

Mellanby, H., *Animal Life in Fresh Water*, Methuen, 1963

O'Reilley, P., *Matching the Hatch*, Swan Hill Press, 1997

Price, T., *Tying and Fishing the Sedge*, Blandford, 1994

Price, T., *Tying and Fishing the Nymph*, Blandford, 1995

Roberts, J., *Trout on a Nymph*, Crowood Press, 1991

Roberts, J., *A Guide to River Trout Flies*, Crowood Press, 1989

Roberts, J., *New Illustrated Dictionary*, Allen and Unwin, 1988

Ronalds, A., *The Fly-Fisher's Entomology* (1836), Flyfishers Classic Library, 1993

Stuart, M., *Herbs and Herbalism*, Book Club Association, 1985

Various, *Field Guide to the Wild Flowers of Britain*, Reader's Digest, 1995

Various Publications, Freshwater Biological Association

Index

Index

Index